for Anne Stevenson

I would like to express my thanks to Angela Topping, John Farrell and Nevil Jones for their encouragement and friendship but most especially to Professor John Lucas without whom so much …

WISE HEREAFTER

Observations on
Shakespeare's *The Tempest*

Matt Simpson

GREENWICH EXCHANGE
LONDON

Greenwich Exchange, London

First published in Great Britain in 2004
Reprinted 2005
All rights reserved

Printed and bound by Q3 Digital/Litho, Loughborough
Tel: 01509 213456
Typesetting and layout by Albion Associates, London
Tel: 020 8852 4646
Cover design by December Publications, Belfast
Tel: 028 90286559

Cover photograph © John Timbers / Arena PAL

Greenwich Exchange Website: www.greenex.co.uk

ISBN 1-871551-75-7

A magician in his art and yet not damnable.

As You Like It

*Some, when they take Revenge, are more desirous
the Party should know, whence it commeth. This is
the more Generous For the Delight seemeth to be,
not so much in doing the Hurt as in Making the
Party Repent.*

Francis Bacon

*He who wishes to avenge his injuries by returning
hate for hate cannot fail to be unhappy. He, on the
other hand, who endeavours to combat hatred with
love, finds in this struggle both joy and security ...
He has less need than any one of Fortune's aid.*

Spinoza

*And all the host of heaven shall be dissolved, and
the heavens shall be folden like a book ... The
Heavens shall pass away with a noyse, and the
elements shall melt with heate, and the earth with all
the works therein, shall be burnt up.*

Isaiah

Contents

Prologue – As in a Dream

One of William Blake's *Proverbs of Hell* states "What is now proved was once only imagin'd". That word "only", from someone who extolled the primacy of the imagination, is, I am convinced, meant to be sarcastic. Blake is scorning what in the same set of proverbs he calls "the horses of instruction", those who seek to explain things with single vision, a mode of perception described by John Beer in his *Blake's Humanism* as "a state of Darkness ... in which un-illuminated Reason alone holds sway." I am beginning on this note because I think it necessary to provide ourselves with a warning against looking for a simple equation to 'explain' *The Tempest*, Shakespeare's most elusive and, in many ways, most puzzling play. In it Shakespeare, time and time again, transgresses the line between what is real and what is imagined, so much so that what is real and what is imagined can both become problematic. This is a play whose truths are multi-layered, one in which how we perceive and with whose eyes we do so are constantly being challenged. Multiple perspectives, not single vision, are required. I am reminded of similar challenges offered by Kurosawa's great film, *Rashamon*, and Lawrence Durrell's sequence of novels called *The Alexandrian Quartet,* in which we are required to consider the same story from a variety of viewpoints.

Shakespeare's island is an imagined place, a science-fiction of its day, as were islands and countries conjured up in traveller's tales. It is perhaps not too difficult for us to see it as a sort of *Star Trek*, in which the island is the interplanetary spacecraft with Prospero as Captain Kirk/Pickard, Ariel as Data and Caliban as having some likenesses to Warf. (An interesting sci-fi film version was made in 1956, starring Walter Pidgeon, called *Forbidden Planet,* of which *The New Yorker* quipped "It's a pity they didn't lift some of Shakespeare's language.") If we push the artificial intelligence idea far enough we might even see Ariel and Caliban as experimental robotic models created by Prospero. Better this than having them appear on stage as quasi-pantomime or Disney figures: Ariel the twee fairy on the Christmas tree and Caliban an old rolled-up tattered carpet. The play requires us to honour their species of consciousness too.

What we conjure up and what Shakespeare's audience may have imagined are in many respects different things. Their imaginations, for example, were more readily fired by the excitements of classical mythology. Let's note that Greek culture (the product, to some degree, of an *island* people) and Roman culture both find their locus in the Mediterranean. Homer and Virgil wrote epics about Mediterranean island-hopping heroes and it was believed, certainly in medieval times, that a kinsman of Aeneas (a survivor of Troy), one Felix Brutus, had actually founded the kingdom of Britain. Much of this culture was mediated to them through the products of Renaissance Italy and by the 'idea' of Italy, towards which country-of-the-mind Shakespeare's audience almost certainly had an ambivalent attitude: it was a focus of Renaissance wonderment and of glories they wished to emulate, while at the same time it was a place of Machiavellian intrigue and sensational murder. All of this was a living part of their imagined world.

For them the sea, for example, was 'peopled' and governed by gods, goddesses and nymphs. How 'real', we can legitimately ask, are such beings when they are (only) imagined? They were not (merely) ornamental but beings that find themselves consistently brought to life and given a contemporary relevance in plays, pageants, paintings, tapestries, poetry and prose. They were part of the glory of the world, a compendium of magical and moral-bearing stories – high among them being Ovid's *Metamorphoses*, a favourite of Shakespeare, whose influence on *The Tempest,* a play of transformations, is palpable.

Additionally, the imaginations of Shakespeare's time were stocked with biblical stories (with regard to the sea, there is Jonah, Noah, St Paul's shipwreck on Malta, etc.) Intuition tells me that Shakespeare had the *Book of Isaiah* somewhere at the back of his mind in writing this play. The name Ariel, for instance, derives from there ("WOE to Ariel, to Ariel, the city *where* David dwelt" – though Shakespeare is clearly attracted to the name for its association with 'air' and 'airiness'). *Isaiah* is concerned with futures through prophecy (this is part of the fabric of the play). In *Shakespeare's Comic Sequence* Muir quotes chapter 34, verse 4 from what is the Geneva Bible used in Shakespeare's time (that is until the Authorised Version of 1611, coincidentally the date of play, replaced it):

> And all the host of heaven shall be dissolved, and the heavens shall be folden like a book ... The Heavens shall passe away with a noyse, and the elements shall melt with heate, and the earth with all the works that are therein, shall be burnt up.

Chapter 54, verse 11 (I have only the James I Bible to hand) gives us:

> O thou afflicted, tossed with tempest, and not comforted, behold, I will lay thy stones with fair colours and lay thy foundations with sapphires.

In his *Shakespeare: the Invention of the Human*, Harold Bloom quotes chapter 47, verse 1, which concerns the destruction of Babylon when he discusses the puns being made on 'temperance' in Act II, scene 1:

> Come downe and sit in the dust: a virgine, daughter Babel, sit on the grounde: there is no throne, O daughter of the Chaldeans: for thou shalt no more be called, Tendre and delicate.

A Bible Concordance gives 18 references to 'tempest', 'tempest-tossed', 'tempestuous'.

On top of these there were exciting contemporary reports of seafarers' expeditions, such as those of William Strachey and Sylvester Jourdain, to which *The Tempest*, as we know, is directly indebted. Enthusiasm for reading the adventures of seafarers was well-catered for by the publications of Richard Hakylut, who started collecting and publishing such accounts from 1582. His major work was *Principall Navigations, Voiages, and Discoveries of the English Nation* of 1589, which he enlarged in three volumes between 1589 and 1600. Jan Kott, in *Shakespeare Our Contemporary*, makes the simple point that at this time "everyone had to realise the earth was round and now twice the size."

Not only the classical, biblical, and accounts of sea-dog expeditions – the audience attended *theatres*, in which pacts were made between audience and performance to enter imaginary worlds. One of these, The Globe, whose motto was "All the World's a Stage", was Shakespeare's "wooden O", a place of illusion: it represented and brought imaginatively to life the world beyond it – just as islands relate to mainlands beyond them. (Voyages join Prospero's island to Italy and to North Africa and therefore the play may well have, between its lines, things to say about the political, religious, trade nexus of Christians and Moors. Alonso, remember, has married his daughter, Claribel – against advice – to an African). And yet the theatre was, as Shakespeare keeps reminding his audience, (only) a "wooden O", a "cockpit" ... though able to hold (with its audience's 'imaginary forces' at work) the "vasty fields of France". This "wooden O" was an arena where actors (often called 'shadows') played parts – sometimes pretending to be actors playing parts, as in a play-within-a-play – who then, like the audience, went home as themselves to cakes and ale. As E.M.W. Tillyard, in *Shakespeare's Last Plays* says of the masque in *The Tempest,* "On the actual stage the masque is executed by players pretending to be spirits, pretending to be real actors, pretending to be supposed goddesses and rustics". (It is almost certain that developments in stage machinery and lighting that went with the presentation of masques and functioned in the then recently-acquired indoor theatre at Blackfriars may have influenced certain effects in *The Tempest.*) The theatre was for its couple of hours' "traffic of our stage" a microcosm containing, like Chinese boxes, other microcosms – in our case a ship, an island and the mind of man.

The island also related to other literary islands. Utopian visions are not too far from mind – Sir Thomas More's, Montaigne's (directly called upon in *The Tempest* – more, in the words of Harold Bloom, as "provocation than source"), and the idealised landscapes of Romance literature in such works as Sidney's *Arcadia* – and behind these the classical myth of the Golden Age and the biblical story of the Garden of Eden. John Hale in *The Civilization of Europe in the Renaissance* describes what he calls "the civilized nostalgia for the Golden Age" in the following way:

It drew on the vision of medieval millenarianism: a world of restored simplicity in which man, naked amidst the ruins of his pomps and institutions, awaited judgement. It was quickened by reports of the Amerindians who 'seem to lyve in the goulden worlde ... wherin men lyved simplye and innocentlye', as the English translator in 1533 of Peter Martyr's *On the New World* phrased it, and was sustained by what was seen as a corruption of an originally natural way of life. The Myth of the Golden Age came to be hymned by court poets at ease in their sinecures, and was embodied at great cost by devisers of princely pageants. It evoked from Montaigne a deeply felt nostalgia for a lost state of nature; it induced Cervantes, and not only for comic effect, to make Sancho Panza resign the cares of governorship of which he was at first so proud; and it produced (mediated through Florio's translation of Montaigne's essay *On the Cannibals*) Gonzalo's anti-civility speech in *The Tempest* ... The fashion for this sort of yearning was already so diffused by 1566 that the French philosopher Jean Bodin judged that it warranted a snub; he pointed out that it was subversive and foolish, undermining civilized values. It romanticized a time 'in which men were scattered like beasts in the fields and the woods and had as much as they could keep by means of force and crime, until gradually they were reclaimed from that ferocity and barbarity to the refinement of customs and the law-abiding society which we see about us'.

During the presentation of the masque, Ferdinand, overwhelmed by "a most majestic vision", declares:

> Let me live here ever!
> So rare a wondered father and a wise
> Makes this place Paradise.
>
> (Act IV, scene 1, 122-4)

It was, then, an imagined space, like Crusoe's island, like Swift's Laputa, the island of *Lord of the Flies* – one containing worlds within worlds and belonging, as Muir says, to "the frontier between ethics and aesthetics, between the real world and the imagined world of art".

The world Shakespeare lived through was subject, like all eras, to inspiring and unsettling changes. The theatre was undergoing a change of fashion: tragic-comedy was replacing the earlier vogue for tragedy; the known world was expanding; the cosmological order (the way the universe was understood) was radically shifting when telescopes were invented. The geocentric universe was threatened with being replaced by a heliocentric one; men made voyages that expanded the boundaries of the known world; there were new continents, strange islands inhabited by strange unchristian people; men dreamed of flight, painted astonishing pictures; they dreamed of inventing war-machines, transposing base metals into gold; they created beautiful buildings; they underwent religious wars, burnt people at the stake, endured visitations of the plague, attended wonderful plays but also watched bear- and bull-baiting, and gruesome public executions; scholars across Europe (Copernicus, Erasmus, Galileo, John Dee, etc.) visited each other and exchanged stirring thoughts, pursued scientific ideas that eventually came to shape our modern world; great artists, poets and philosophers set about describing and depicting the world as they saw it and as they imagined it. Jan Kott calls *The Tempest* "a drama of men of the Renaissance" and lists among the play's themes a critique of the philosophical utopia, the limits of human experience, the unity of man and nature, and the dangers threatening the moral order. For him, the play is "serious and severe, lyrical and grotesque ... a drama of lost illusions, bitter wisdom, and of fragile – though stubborn – hope".

It is worth reminding ourselves that whenever we see the play acted the production we experience will already have certain givens (production values), pre-determining how we see and understand it. For example, one director may decide that Prospero is a benevolent, white magician (the conventional view); another might see his "rough magic" as dangerous dabbling in the black arts. Again, a director will decide that the villains Antonio and Sebastian either join in the circle of forgiveness at the end or bluntly refuse to do so. Such productions will offer interpretations which our own reading of the text may or may not wish to sanction. As John Wain says in *The Living World of Shakespeare,* "a fireside reader, if he wishes to get the best out of any Shakespeare play, will always mount a stage-production in the theatre of his mind: he will always be ready to say definitely what, at any given moment, he would instruct an actor or actress to *do*." This may, as I have suggested, prove problematic when we see the play on the stage: it is certainly a problem lecturers and teachers (who may become overly attached to their own notions built up and stuck to over a number of years) may have to confront.

We need to remind ourselves how impossible it is for us to see Shakespeare's works with innocent eyes, i.e. as his original audiences did, who, if they were first-timers, would not (like those of us who are over-familiar) know what was *going-to-happen-next*. For example, take the scene in *The Winter's Tale* in which a statue comes to life: the play gives no hint that this is to happen; it is a stunningly theatrical moment, but one diminished if we *already know* the plot. Our responses are complicated by the fact that we also look with the eyes of a different culture and, obviously, from a different point in time. This means we have to make efforts of adjustment if, as Wain says, we are to get the best out of reading Shakespeare.

I am not, of course, saying that any particular interpretation may not be valid, only that some may be more valid than others. Those which distort or rearrange the text or wilfully ignore or override what is clearly the case in it can perhaps be tolerated (and even, in the spirit of the play, forgiven) as long as we feel that Shakespeare himself might have been intrigued or amused.

1

What Is The Time O' Th' Day?

The Tempest is the only one of Shakespeare's plays to obey the classical unities of time, place and action, according to the prescriptions which theorists of the time – notably Sir Philip Sidney in his *Apologie for Poetrie* of 1595 (following what he thought were precepts of Aristotle) – wished upon the drama. It is as if, after a long career in the theatre, Shakespeare is showing the world and those sticklers for 'rules' that he can do the classical if he wants. As Kenneth Muir puts it, "the poet demonstrates it is not through incompetence that he has gone (previously) against Sidney's advice." In *The Winter's Tale*, possibly written the same year as *The Tempest*, Shakespeare brings on (at the start of Act IV) a Chorus personifying Time, who unashamedly states that 16 years have now elapsed. The speech even has a boastful tone to it:

> Impute it not a crime
> To me, or my swift passage, that I slide
> O'er sixteen years, and leave the growth untried
> Of that wide gap, since it is in my pow'r
> To o'erthrow law, and in one self-born hour
> To plant and o'erwhelm custom.
>
> (Act IV, scene 1, 4-9)

Unity of place is, of course, the island; unity of time is four hours of one day, the latter made possible by "the account of the past in the second scene" (Muir); unity of action residing in Prospero's control of events, which is, as Muir points out, "also the poet's".

In performance, the play takes just a little over two hours. The opening storm-scene is over in under five minutes ... and I, for one, am usually glad it takes no longer, since almost all the productions I have watched start badly with a babble of shouting against impossible wind-machines and groaning timbers, with the effect that we experience only a snatched-at handful of the words. I'm not implying that some productions (nor that Shakespeare's company wouldn't have done it properly) can't make it work so that the confusion, panic and tensions are felt as real. But when sound effects overpower the words we miss important themes, which are adumbrated in the scene.

It is shortly after the storm subsides and Prospero has spent twenty minutes in conversation with Miranda that he asks Ariel what the time is. Ariel replies "Past the mid season" (i.e. mid-day) which Prospero glosses with:

> At least two glasses. The time 'twixt six and now
> Must by us both be spent most preciously.
>
> (Act I, scene 2, 240-1)

In other words, it's after two o'clock and Prospero's plans have four hours before hopefully coming to fruition. Part of the illusion then is that the time of the action of the play is twice the time it takes to perform. There is imagined time (duration) and chronological time. Jan Kott suggests that six o'clock was the time performances normally finished and theatres closed. This is interesting: Prospero (as well as the actor playing him) tells the audience in the *Epilogue* that it's time to applaud ("with the help of your good hands") and, the spell thus broken, time to go home. Illusion and reality at this point meet head on. We are both in the imagined space of the play and outside it at the same time. Or at least preparing to disengage from it.

In Act III, scene 1, with about an hour's playing time left, Miranda tells Ferdinand "My father/Is hard at study; pray now rest yourself;/ He's safe these three hours." Act V begins with Prospero again asking Ariel the time, who tells him:

> On the sixth hour, at which time, my lord,
> You said our work should cease.
>
> (Act V, scene 1, 4-5)

With under two hundred lines of the play left, Alonso, asking Prospero for explanations, says:

> If thou beest Prospero,
> Give us particulars of thy preservation;
> How thou hast met us here, whom three hours since
> Were wracked upon this shore;
>
> (Act V, scene 1, 134-7)

A few minutes later he confirms this sense of a three-hour duration by asking his son, Ferdinand:

> What is this maid with whom thou wast at play?
> Your eld'st acquaintance cannot be three hours.
>
> (Act V, scene 1, 185-6)

The Boatswain, too, reports:

> The best news is that we have safely found
> Our King and company; the next, our ship –
> Which, but three glasses since, we gave out split –
> Is tight and yare and bravely rigged, as when
> We first put out to sea.
>
> (Act V, scene 1, 221-5)

Four hours have strangely turned into three and are being imagined in two. Shakespeare may conform to the unities but what he does within them actually confounds our notions of time and space. Ariel defies the laws of time, space and gravity, and can, like Puck in *A Midsummer Night's Dream*, do things (let's recall that one midnight he was called up "to fetch dew/From the still-vex'd Bermoothes") in "a twink". In the final scene he is required to wake the master and the boatswain, out in the harbour, and "enforce them to this place". He says:

> I drink the air before me, and return
> Or ere your pulse beat twice.
>
> (Act V, scene 1, 102-3)

He is back just over a hundred lines later.

To Caliban and Ferdinand, engaged in burdensome chores, time moves differently, more slowly – that is if time is paced by how we perceive it. How is time experienced in madness or in the throes of intoxication? Or in sleep? (Dreams do not obey the laws of time.)

Remember that Prospero can freeze time and make other characters fall asleep against their wills.

One might claim, not too fancifully, that in *The Tempest*, Shakespeare is at his most ludic; that in this last play, he is playing an elaborate theatrical game (Bloom calls the play "a wildly experimental comedy"), pulling out all the stops, and, like Prospero, expectantly putting on a dazzling performance. If he is saying goodbye to the theatre (and who is so hard-boiled as not to want it so?) it is not just in the "cloud-capp'd towers" speech nor the *Epilogue* he is doing so: the whole play (in it he is a "king of infinite space") can perhaps be seen as a gift to his audience and colleagues, the gift of a "most majestic vision", not as something necessarily sad and wistful. (Jan Kott tells us "one has to be blind not to see it in moving personal accents"). In saying this, I am not, of course, denying the play's seriousness: its darker side will be looked at later.

There are other matters involving awareness of time in the play. The past exists only in the present: in Act I scene 2 Prospero tells Miranda "The hour's now come" for her to acquire her own history and so he proceeds to deliver an account of it, attempting in the process to reactivate memories in her, to have her look into "the dark backward and abysm of time". Though he has educated her, he has waited many years for this moment to furnish her with her own truth. Twelve years in fact. And as she was "not/out three years old", we may assume that she is now 15 (Prospero is three times her age and Shakespeare himself was of similar age in 1611). Twelve appears again in the number of years Ariel was penned up in a cloven pine. We cannot know how long after arriving on the island it was that Sycorax punished Ariel this way but it does tell us that Caliban must be at least 24 years old. Numbers to Shakespeare's audience would have magical or symbolic properties. The day for instance is divided into two twelves; there are 12 months in a year etc, etc. We nowadays pay little heed to these mystical and symbolic values (though it is worth noting that it is only through numbers that computers work their 'magic'). Control of numbers is a way of creating and controlling time and therefore of great significance to people like magicians and doctors whose activities involve astrological observations and mathematical calculation. In the time of Shakespeare there was much reliance on horoscopes (involving numbers connected crucially with a person's time of birth – the hour, day, month, year) as a way of forecasting or determining the future: in matters of health (or when best to do something or best to avoid doing it), doctors always cast horoscopes. Religion too made and still makes much use of number symbolism and we must always remember that Shakespeare's audience would automatically see and judge events in what I have called elsewhere the context of eternity. Their thinking was typically analogical too, constantly assuming connections, correspondences and contrasts between things. For example, the masculine, golden sun in the day, the feminine, silver moon at night, the moon influencing the sea and affecting minds with madness. Love's beginnings were seen as a madness, sharing the inconstancy of the moon, which also inspired the divine madness of poetry. The sea serves as an image of time, likewise voyages across it.

It is obvious that the actions of *The Tempest*, like those of navigation, involve mathematical calculation. Prospero has carefully studied and prepared himself for this moment; if he misses it everything goes awry. He tells his daughter:

> Know thus far forth.
> By accident most strange, bountiful Fortune,
> Now my dear lady, hath mine enemies
> Brought to this shore; and by my prescience
> I find my zenith doth depend upon
> A most auspicious star, whose influence
> If now I court not, but omit, my fortunes
> Will ever after droop.
>
> (Act I, scene 2, 177-84)

One further point – and one that looks like an anomaly – on two occasions Prospero promises Ariel will be free in two days. Is Ariel made free at and by the end of the play? The words of his master:

> My Ariel, chick,
> That is thy charge. Then to the elements
> Be free, and fare thou well.
>
> (Act V, scene 1, 317-19)

make it sound as though it is going to take two days to arrange "calm seas, auspicious gales,/And sail so expeditious, that shall catch/ (the) royal fleet far off"? But then Prospero invites Alonso and his retinue to spend the night in his cell before setting off for Naples the following morning.

2

Qualities O' Th' Isle

Harold Bloom tells us "perspective governs everything on Prospero's island, which can be seen either as desert or as paradise, depending upon the viewer". If apprehension of time depends on the kind and quality of consciousness perceiving it (it is a truism that the older we get the speedier time seems to travel) then the same may be said for how place is perceived and interpreted. A sense of place is a determining factor in human consciousness. It is rightly said that we are at the centre of an 'out-there' world, and we have the ability to place ourselves accordingly.

It is a matter of significance that characters in *The Tempest* lose their sense of being at the centre of an 'out-there' world and/or have their perceptions of it challenged. All of them, in one way or another, suffer displacement or dislocation. This should be familiar to us as a theme of modern literature, with our keywords alienation and deracination. And each of the characters sees the island differently – whether as a reflection of, and implied moral comment on, their real selves or part of Prospero's spell is not always easy to distinguish … that is unless we suppose the spell makes them, despite themselves, reveal their 'true' selves to the audience or the selves to which they are eventually obliged to wake up. An important speech is Gonzalo's:

> O, rejoice
> Beyond a common joy, and set it down
> With gold on lasting pillars. In one voyage
> Did Claribel her husband find at Tunis,
> And Ferdinand her brother found a wife
> Where he himself was lost; Prospero his dukedom

In a poor isle, and all of us ourselves
When no man was his own.

(Act V, scene 1, 206-213)

A Jungian interpretation of the play would deploy the words 'synchronicity' (a coincidence of events that give the appearance of being related) and 'individuation' (the process of the development of the self, in which conflicts that arise at certain transitional stages in one's life are resolved). A Freudian view, such as that of Maureen Duffy in her book, *The Erotic World of Fairy*, would say that the play deals with the incest taboo from which the daughter (as in so many fairy stories and folk lore) would be rescued by a brother or brothers or by a hero-figure. Duffy asserts that "The island is the forbidden world of (Prospero's) relationship with Miranda" and that his "return and renunciation of magic power are synonymous with finding a husband for his daughter". This power, she insists, is "a father's dominating influence and his magic the parent's seeming ability in the child's eyes to do anything". The spell he puts upon her is equivalent to 'neurotic catalepsy' – the "inability to move because of the conflict of desire and fear".

Sycorax, pregnant with Caliban, is banished from Algiers and "here left by th' sailors"; she dies on the island within the space of the dozen years Ariel is locked up in the pine; not long after this Prospero, banished from Milan (Shakespeare imagines Milan to be a port), takes refuge there; the Neapolitan King, his retinue (people used to the sophisticated – corrupt – life of the court) and the sailors of his royal ship, en route from Tunis to Naples, are magically thrown up there 12 years later; Ariel suffers dislocation in being confined to a cloven pine for 12 years and then freed only to be kept in thrall to Prospero; goddesses in the form of a court masque incongruously appear on the island; Caliban, once "mine own King", is "usurped" and enslaved by Prospero, until whose arrival:

was this island –

Save for the son that she did litter here,
A freckled whelp, hag-born – not honoured with
A human shape.

(Act I, scene 2, 281-4)

The stage directions to *The Tempest* are unusually detailed, which some people suggest is the result of Shakespeare sending his company the script from Stratford. Be that as it may, we are obviously not to take the stage direction "The scene, an uninhabited island" literally. It contains a spacious cell in which live a father and his daughter; Caliban lives on the island too (note that according to Miranda in Act I, scene 2 he is one of the three *men* "that e'er I saw"); and it is haunted by spirits. The word "uninhabited" suggests a wild place (an imagined one) and therefore takes us beyond the bounds of civilisation into the world of untamed nature ... though it is also the location of experiments with nurture: the education of Miranda and the failed attempt to civilise Caliban. This is a theme to be touched on later.

Scholars have fruitlessly tried to locate the island geographically. It is an *imagined* island which, as Kott says, is at the same time "the whole world". "It is useless," he rightly states, "to look for the longitude and latitude of Prospero's island". It does not, except as the setting for a play in performance, belong on any map or in chronological time. Fixing it as Malta or an island near Sicily or off the coast of North Africa is a game that gets us nowhere. The fact that Ariel whizzes off to the Bermudas and Sycorax's god was Setebos, a Patagonian deity, should warn us against taking its Mediterranean setting too literally, as confining. (This is not to say that an implicit Mediterranean culture and politics at the time of the first production should be undervalued. Hulme and Sherman in their edition of a collection of essays, *The Tempest and Its Travels*, make the point that "it has always been possible to argue that Shakespeare's various geographies were indicative of his interest in other worlds rather than the perceived need for artistic conventions that enabled the staging of issues too close to home for the comfort of the playwright and his company.")

The island provides useful commodities and at the same time things of little use – having salt and fresh water, fertile and barren ground, rocks, caves, angles, a harbour, fruit trees and quagmires; on it grow hazelnuts, lemons, apples (crab apples), berries, thorns, truffles; it is home to a strange menagerie of hedgehogs, baboons, snakes, bats, bears, toads; we hear dogs barking and reports of bulls and lions roaring and cocks crowing (a place of noises as well as music). But it is, above all, a testing ground, literally and symbolically, a stage upon which crucial events are being played out. To Prospero it is the place Providence landed him 12 years before; it is a grateful alternative to death in Milan or at sea; it is where he can, through the kindness and prescience of old Gonzalo, continue his studies, protect and educate his daughter; it is the focus of all his hopes and the culmination of his studies, which will eventually restore his dukedom to him and marry his daughter to the heir apparent of the kingdom of Naples. It is where space and time are nervously controlled: as with navigators, the calculations have to come out right, the proper signs have to be evident, if Fortune and "accident most strange" are to deliver his enemies up to him. Prospero's magic is not absolute: it is dependent upon his getting his sums right. The name Prospero, if we look to its Latin derivation, suggests not just prosperity (someone who has profited) but more importantly, if we read 'spero' as 'I hope' and 'pro' to suggest 'in the future', then there are other resonances available to us. Prospero associated only with prosperity becomes an automatic goodie, whereas 'hope for the future' determines something quite different: an excited concentration (it is the excitement that may be felt with any creative enterprise) on calculations being right and coincident with providence. This allows for a degree of dramatic tension and it accounts for Prospero's occasional bursts of temper and moodiness. To him the island is a magic circle, a place of banishment turned into a place of judgement and redress.

To Miranda (as we would expect from her name) the island is a place of much wonder and also of patience in which her formative years are spent; it is her university; a place of molested but preserved virginity; it is the trysting place, where she meets her true love and becomes betrothed. It is where she obeys her father and then, like Desdemona, disobeys him when her heart has gone elsewhere. She tells Ferdinand her name and quickly admits:

> O my father,
> I have broke your hest to say so!
>
> (Act III, scene 1, 37-8)

and some twenty-odd lines later confesses:

But I prattle
Something too wildly, and my father's precepts
I therein do forget.

(Act III, scene 1, 57-9)

This feels like a parody of events in the Garden of Eden ... man's first disobedience! I say 'parody' because in the context of the play, like the wrangle over chess (another instance of dissension), it feels to be more an aspect of Miranda's innocence than anything deeply culpable.

To Ariel the island is where he is free and where he is in service: free to defy the laws of gravity and time. He cannot therefore complain he has no freedom of movement or even of choice – he had, after all, refused to act Sycorax's "earthy and abhorr'd commands". The "pains" he complains of are not, like those of Caliban, physical hurts but simply difficult tasks of organisation and timing. He owes gratitude and loyalty to Prospero and, though impatient for complete freedom, fulfils his master's "grand behests ... To every article". For 12 years, the island was his place of imprisonment. His ultimate freedom when it comes is to the elements – the upwardly mobile elements of air and fire with which he is throughout the play associated.

Caliban experiences the island as a place of servitude, physical pain and failure – failure to take advantage of learning and in allowing what glimpse he has of love to be betrayed by lust. It is experienced physically (he is "styed" in a hard rock) in the carrying of logs and other duties, also as sexual frustration and an agonising awareness of beauty he cannot possess or do anything about, except in frustration, violate. This is not just Miranda: it is also something he often experiences as tantalisingly beautiful music:

Be not afeard; the isle is full of noises,
Sounds, and sweet airs, that give delight and hurt not.
Sometimes a thousand twangling instruments
Will hum about mine ears; and sometime voices,
That, if I then had waked after long sleep,
Will make me sleep again; and, then, in dreaming,
The clouds methought would open, and show riches

11

Ready to drop on me, that, when I waked
I cried to dream again.

(Act III, scene 2, 137-145)

It is also a place of resentments: he thinks of himself as an usurped king of the island:

This island's mine, by Sycorax my mother,
Which thou tak'st from me.

(Act I, scene 2, 331-2)

as well as a place of capitulation. "I must eat my dinner," he says, knowing he is dependent upon Prospero, whose magic he cannot answer, for food and shelter:

I must obey. His art is of such power,
It would control my dam's god Setebos,
And make a vassal of him.

(Act I, scene 2, 372-4)

Ferdinand, sometimes too easily played as a kind of Prince Charming, finds the island a place of puzzling enchantment, where music strangely "allays ... fury and ... passion", where he meets what he thinks is a goddess, one he is delighted to subsequently find is human and a virgin (we will consider the importance of virginity and chastity in the play later); it is also a hard-labour prison, but one he willingly endures for the sake of love; it is also therefore a place where, in love, he, like a knight undergoing an ordeal, – as happens in the comedies – has to pass a test. During the masque, as we have said, he thinks of it as a Paradise.

To the king and his retinue it is a maze that mixes straight and winding paths, a place of loss, death, survival, madness, fear; an arena in which self-discovery of guilt is managed, a place of judgement, as we have already stated, and redress; it is a limbo in which their souls have to earn reprieve. Sebastian and Antonio see it as an unwholesome fen; to them the ground is tawny (to Gonzalo it is lush, lusty, green); it is also where they continue displaying their habitual court cynicism, the use (or abuse) of wit to plume up their wills and enjoy the discomfort of others; and, as they are opportunists, a place for possible political assassination. The irony, of course, is that they do not realise they have been dumped on an island with no ostensible prospect of return to Italy and that their machinations are therefore politically pointless. Adrian is confused: he thinks the island a "desert ... uninhabitable and almost inaccessible" while acknow-ledging the climate "subtle, tender and delicate" and that the "air breathes upon us here most sweetly". (This may be an in-joke: in other plays Shakespeare seems in-jokingly to complain about the smelliness of the audience). Gonzalo looks about him to find whatever comfort there might be. It allows him (a strategy aimed at cheering and consoling Alonso) a utopian flight of fancy, which shows us that Shakespeare has been reading the essays of Montaigne.

To the king, fearing the death of his son, it is a place of sad loss, a loss compounded by the thought he has also, by putting a great distance between them, lost his daughter. It is a place where words lose their meaning for him.

Trinculo and Stephano suffer a renewal of the storm; they fear the island superstitiously, imagining (not without some irony) it to be the abode of devils and monsters. They import drunkenness into it, riotous behaviour, and, like Antonio and Sebastian, are tempted to effect murder, though are easily distracted by the glittering apparel hanging on the line. Even Caliban can see the stupidity of this distraction. He worships Stephano as the king of the island (to whom it becomes "a brave kingdom"); it is a place in which they can, in an unwittingly beautiful phrase, "smell music" whilst at the same time "smell all horsepiss".

In the end, the island becomes a place to leave and in the *Epilogue* reverts to being a wooden stage from which an actor addresses the audience directly. Prospero and the actor playing him abandon "this bare island" (an empty stage) and sail away on the breath (the good report) of the audience ... as far as tomorrow's performance and another sea of faces.

An amusing slant to the view of Prospero as actor is given by Northrop Frye (quoted by Harold Bloom) who imagines Prospero as a:

> harassed overworked actor-manager, scolding lazy actors,
> praising the good ones in connoisseur's language, thinking
> up jobs for the idle, constantly aware of his limited time before
> his show goes on, his nerves tense and alert for breakdowns
> while it is going on, looking forward to a peaceful retirement,

yet in the meantime having to go out and beg the audience for applause.

It is the romantic in me that wants to see Prospero/Shakespeare as more seriously playful and it is the realist (as well as the fantasist) who would endorse Kott's choice of Hieronymus Bosch (thinking of his *Garden of Earthly Delights*) as the painter to put it on canvas.

3

The Salt Deep

To state the obvious, an island is an island by virtue of its surrounding sea. The sea isolates, and islands can only be come upon by men voyaging in ships. Robert Foulke, in an essay entitled *The Literature of Voyaging*, has this to say:

> We embark on voyages not only to get somewhere but also to accomplish something, and along the way to discover ourselves and our prospects in the world. In this sense voyages are a natural vehicle for the human imagination exploring the unknown, whether it be discovering new continents, finding out the truth about oneself, or reaching those more perfect worlds we call utopias.

The Tempest involves three voyages and the prospect of another: sailors bring the pregnant Sycorax from Algiers, because of her "mischiefs manifold, and sorceries terrible", and maroon her on the island; Prospero, having neglected "all worldly ends, all dedicated/ To closeness and the bettering" of his mind, is, with his three-year-old daughter, providentially thrown up there after a journey from Naples made in a "rotten carcass of a butt"; the King and his retinue are magically brought to it when on their way back from Tunis to Naples (a reminder of Mediterranean political polarities – such as we find in *Othello* – between Moors and Christians and connections between Spain and Italy); and the play ends with Prospero's declaration to Alonso that:

> in the morn,
> I'll bring you to your ship, and so to Naples,
> Where I have hope to see the nuptial
> Of these our dear-beloved solemnized;

And thence retire me to my Milan, where
Every third thought shall be my grave.

(Act V, scene 1, 307-12)

The first two of these voyages are banishments, alternatives to mainland deaths: Sycorax escapes execution because of her pregnancy ("for one thing she did/They would not take her life"); Prospero, asked by Miranda why Antonio did not "That hour destroy us?" is told:

Dear, they durst not,
So dear the love my people bore me; nor set
A mark so bloody on the business.

(Act I, scene 2, 140-2)

The third ends in self-discovery and in the opening up of prospects. each of these voyages also tempts the imagination, not only with spirits and magical events but also with "those more perfect worlds we call utopias".

There is a sense too in which Prospero has been intellectually voyaging for 12 years, waiting, as it were, for his ship to come home. The promised voyage at the end of the play restores an order disrupted a dozen years earlier, one in which we set sail out beyond the play. Is Kott right in saying "Prospero agrees to return to Milan. In this alone lies the difficult and precarious optimism of *The Tempest*"? It is something we shall consider later.

The words of Psalm 107 would be familiar to Shakespeare and his audience. I quote verses 23-30 in the James I translation:

23 They that go down to the sea in ships, that do business in great waters;

24 They see the works of the LORD, and his wonders in the deep

25 For he commandeth, and raiseth the stormy wind, which lifteth the waves thereof.

26 They mount up to the heaven, they go down again to the depths: their soul is melted because of trouble

27 They reel to and fro, and stagger like a drunken man,
and are at their wits' end.

28 Then they cry unto the LORD in their trouble, and he
bringeth them out of their distresses.

29 He maketh the storm a calm, so that the waves thereof
are still.

30 Then are they glad because they be quiet; so he bringeth
them unto their desired haven.

This is almost a template for the plot of *The Tempest* – that is if
we see Prospero acting as – or as the agent of – the Lord. It contains
some of the interplay of opposites that informs the play: control and
lack of it, mounting up and going down, heavens and depths, violent
storm and calm delivery, power and submission, order and disorder
(to include madness and drunkenness), sorrow and joy.

It is frequently pointed out that *The Tempest* is unique in beginning
with a storm. In Shakespeare's other plays, storms (or their
equivalents, war, madness, drunkenness, the vagaries of young love)
more often attend the climax and serve as a rite of passage. Is
Shakespeare/Prospero seeking a calm of mind, all passion spent?
"He maketh the storm a calm so that the waves thereof are still." (A
further parallel may be found in *Luke*, Chapter 8 where we learn that
Jesus, with his disciples on board a ship, falls asleep and a storm
blows up; the disciples wake him and he stills the raging winds:
"Then he arose, and rebuked the wind and the raging of the water:
and they ceased and there was calm. And he said unto them, Where
is your faith? And they being afraid wondered, saying one to another,
What manner of man is this! for he commandeth even the winds and
water, and they obeyed him.")

According to Muir, the sea in the play is "an important symbol of
separation and estrangement". This is obviously true (Claribel
"dwells/Ten leagues beyond man's life") but the sea is other things
too. It threatens life and can quickly take it away; it can rage, swallow
and cast up; it can, with the help of providence, preserve life; it is
indifferent to feudal distinction ("What care these roarers for the
name of king?"); it is, through salt tears, associated with sorrow; it

can stain garments; be beautiful and ugly, an obstacle, a place of discoveries and of new life; it can inspire awe and compassion (as in Miranda's "O, I have suffered/With those that I saw suffer!"); inspire superstition as well as a righteous fear of the Almighty; it can be a proving ground for heroes (Odysseus, Aeneas, Jason, Columbus, Drake, Raleigh, et al); it requires navigational mathematics to traverse it. And, as we said earlier, it is 'peopled' with gods, goddesses and nymphs ("Sea nymphs hourly ring his knell"). It is also a great creator of transformations, magically metamorphosing bones into coral, eyes into pearls; and, like the god Proteus, it is itself forever changing shape. Transformation is a key theme of the Christian religion. As it says in *1 Corinthians*, "Look! I tell you a sacred secret. We shall not all fall asleep (in death), but we shall all be changed, in a moment, in the twinkling of an eye, during the last trumpet." (The phrase "twinkling of an eye" may remind us of Ariel's abilities to perform things in "a twink"). The island is a place where transformations into "something rich and strange" are constantly in progress. The sea of the play, like the island, belongs to and exists in the imagination. The sea is the audience. And that audience is a London audience. John Hale reminds us:

Our knowledge of Shakespeare is scant for three reasons: the thinness of documentary evidence for his life; the avoidance of overtly personal viewpoints in his plays; and the perennial mystery of the nature of genius. But ... it would be impossible to get even near to the sources of his inspiration without seeing him as a lip-reader of the conversational encyclopaedia that London represented, with its range of educated acquaintance open to a fashionable actor and author, its tavern raffishness, its status hovering between that of island and continent for those engaged in trade, diplomacy and soldiering, its foreign communities which would provide the local colour for *The Merchant of Venice* and the Franglais of Hal and Katherine's wooing scene in *Henry V*, and encourage the 'Boscos thromuldo boskos' mumbo-jumbo of Parolles' presumed Muscovite captors in *All's Well That Ends Well*.

It is also, as Crystal Bartolovich argues in her essay 'Baseless Fabric: London as a World City', a 'globalized' London. In their Introduction to *The Tempest and Its Travels* in which her essay appears, Hulme and Sherman summarise her thesis as "What signalled London status as a 'world city' by the time of *The Tempest* was not only its increasingly important position as a hub for international trade, but the extent to which its theatre was staging problems of location and identity."

Note:

W.H. Auden's series of lectures given at the University of Virginia in 1949 and published by Faber in 1951 under the title *The Enchafèd Flood,* which takes as its subject 'The Romantic Iconography of the Sea', is a stimulating account of the topic.

4

Potent Art

In the Introduction to his influential 1954 Arden edition of the play, Frank Kermode describes Prospero's art as "the disciplined exercise of virtuous knowledge ... Art is not only a beneficent magic in contrast to an evil one; it is the ordination of civility, the control of appetite, the transformation of nature by breeding and learning; it is even, in this sense, the means of Grace." This, of course, is a perfectly acceptable reading and one that is sustained in the views of many critics and directors. In it we must inevitably see Prospero's 'art' set in contrast to Sycorax's witchcraft and working in opposition to Caliban's "nature"; see it servicing the good and finding ways of controlling the bad and the seemingly unpredictable, and creating conditions in which revenge can be transformed into forgiveness.

Nowadays, since the advent of modern theory and, in particular, colonial studies, when, in the impatient words of Jonathan Bate in *The Genius of Shakespeare*, "the task of literary theory became to assuage the guilt of empire by making the author of *The Tempest* a scapegoat", we are faced with a choice. Bate puts it this way: "A 'Prosperian' reading of the play locates darkness in Caliban's nature; a 'Calibanesque' reading finds it in Prospero's art of nurture which is a means to mastery." Either way, critical allegiances can be stretched. For example, a traditionalist like Harold Bloom understandably takes the view:

> Of all Shakespeare's plays, the two visionary comedies – *A Midsummer Night's Dream* and *The Tempest* – these days share the sad distinction of being the worst interpreted and performed. Erotomania possesses the critics and directors of the *Dream*, while ideology drives the bespoilers of *The Tempest*. Caliban, a poignant but cowardly (and murderous)

half-human (his father a sea-devil, whether fish or amphibian), has become an African-Caribbean heroic Freedom Fighter. This is not even a weak misreading; anyone who arrives at that view is simply not interested in reading the play at all. Marxists, multiculturalists, feminists, *nouveau* historicists – the usual suspects – know their causes but not Shakespeare's plays.

That said, I have seen a production of the play in Australia in which it did not seem improper to point Caliban up as an aboriginal native and have him played by one. As Hulme and Sherman suggest, Caliban is one of a "handful of characters (that) seem to break free of their original text and become culturally available across a wide spectrum." They go on to say that Caliban's "'hunger' has been crucial to the play's renewed power". It is not however unfair to ask – if we take the play to show a relationship between exploiter and exploited – what, other than Caliban, there is to exploit on the island. No resources beyond those that enable its residents to subsist are mentioned – no gold or silver, no spices – and Prospero doesn't *want* to remain there (as an occupying colonial power). He wants, when Fortune smiles on him, to get off it, after a long 12 year exile, and return to his Milan dukedom.

The fact of the matter is that no single reading of the play can do it justice. It is, as we have said earlier, multi-layered. But sometimes it helps to emphasise one aspect at the expense of others so as to make us experience, in having our perspectives challenged, a revitalising of our appreciation of its energies. It is, after all, what the play itself does: challenges perspectives, constantly revitalises. An open mind is what we need. It is a measure of their power that Shakespeare's plays survive even the worst kind of treatments.

An obvious feature of *The Tempest* – so obvious it is often overlooked – is the restraint Shakespeare uses in dramatising Prospero's magic. He refrains from spooking the audience directly with spells, incantations and invocations, as he did in *Macbeth*; gives us no circles, signs, potions, formulae; no indication of what his 'books' actually contain.

Whether he deals in white or black magic is something we will consider shortly. The Romantic in me would like to believe that Shakespeare and his audience had memories of Marlowe's *Dr Faustus*

(Bloom offers the view that Prospero is "Shakespeare's anti-Faust, and a final transcending of Marlowe"), that certain parallels and/or differences came into their minds: Prospero using magic, with the aid of providence, for benevolent purposes (though we will question this later), almost to the point of seeming to assume a God-like role; Faust selling his soul for 24 years of black magic (24 years is the time between the evil Sycorax's being marooned on the island and the moment of the play's action) and acting as the agent of the Devil – and, ironically, turning into nothing much more than a showman; Prospero with choices available to him, Faustus with merely the illusion of choice. Both acquire knowledge and power from books. At the end of Marlowe's play, Faustus, despairing, cries out that he'll burn his books; at the close of *The Tempest* Prospero promises to *drown* his book (we will ask later the question why the singular is used but for the moment let's register the rite of purification by water, as by holy water and the ceremony of baptism and exorcism, in which evil spirits are driven away). Marlowe putting something of his inner self into the character of Faustus; Shakespeare possibly doing something of the same (through a double meaning we may attach to the word 'art') with Prospero.

Maybe the audience also brought to mind men like the real-life Robert Fludd, mathematician and physician, or Dr John Dee, Elizabeth I's doctor/conjuror/magician, whose unstinting quest for the secrets of the universe – what he called "the treasure of heavenly wisdom and knowledge" – and his exploits in alchemical practice and what we would now call the occult make Prospero's magic tame by comparison. Benjamin Woolley's biography of Dee opens up to us a bizarre world of esoteric lore, the summoning up of angels, visions and the use of mystical calculations. Of Dee, Woolley claims that at "the height of his fame he was poised – like Copernicus and Galileo – to become one of the great figures of the Renaissance", someone who "promoted mathematics as the basis of science, anticipated the invention of the telescope and many of Newton's theories, made crucial innovations in cartography and the art of navigation, and created one of the most magnificent libraries in Europe." With such vistas, is it any wonder that Faustus declares "a sound magician is a demi-god"? It is entry into this world of knowledge – much of it dependent on acquiring, studying and compiling the right books – which Prospero tells us he values more than his dukedom. It had, as was the case with Faustus, a dangerous allure. Highly dangerous, in that meddling with spirits involved imperilling the soul, being caught in a diabolical deception, and/or led to accusations of witchcraft and burning at the stake. A dangerous world, as Woolley says, "of 'redye reckonynges' and alchemy". (None of this is to suggest, of course, that Prospero is, as writers like Frances Yates argue, a portrait of Dee – any more than Sycorax is the Dark Lady of the Sonnets or Catherine de Medici!)

Perhaps, just as likely, the audience would bring to mind another practitioner of astrology and medicine, Simon Forman, who left accounts of attendances at some of Shakespeare's plays and who, according to his biographer, A.L. Rowse, supplies the clue to the possible identity of the 'Dark Lady of the Sonnets'. Rowse tells us that:

> Forman was absolutely convinced of the truth of astrology – as other people are of the truth of the doctrines they believe in; he relied upon it for guidance in every aspect of his own affairs and for the course he should take daily, as much as in advising others. If many cases did not work out that was because accuracy could not be obtained, or something had gone wrong with the calculations, difficult and uncertain in any case; or because he did not know enough, and was anxious to learn more. But, then, everybody believed in astrology, more or less. The Queen had her astrologer, Dr Dee, whom she treated with favour; he had cast the horoscope for the most propitious day for her coronation.

Life was governed by the conjunctions and emanations of the sun, moon, planets, zodiac and their harmonious or disharmonious aspects. Rowse says, "It was all part of knowledge, like theology." Forman also "ardently desired, like many Renaissance people, to explore this penumbra" (what we might call the psychic world) "and to gain control over its phenomena – in Elizabethan language, power over the spirits." One wonders what Forman and his like would make of space probes, the Hubble telescope, girdling the earth with satellites, the internet, raising spirits with television.

James I's fascination with witchcraft is well-known and there are records of performances of the play at court in the autumn of 1611 and again a year later as part of the celebrations of the marriage of the King's daughter, Elizabeth, to the Elector Palatine.

Because of the references to Virgil that crop up in the play, the audience would also perhaps know how in popular lore the great Roman poet, Virgil, was seen as a wizard. Dante chose him as a guide through Hell and Purgatory (is Prospero's island a kind of Purgatory?) not only because he was a great poet but because of his supernatural powers. Marina Warner has written that medieval stories tell how Virgil was a wizard "part jester, part necromancer, part prophet, part shaman, a recognisable model for Merlin and Gandalf and even Dumbledore today". Virgil, like the Bible and Montaigne, haunts the lines of *The Tempest*.

Prospero is traditionally considered a white magician (his name, as suggested earlier, can automatically dispose us to think well of him); and if we wish to take the play as a species of pleasant fairy story we will tend to see him as a wise and kindly old man who uses his 'art' to nothing but good purpose. This being the case, the audience, like Miranda, is happy to hear that the storm does no real harm – Prospero giving as his reason for raising it the love he bears his daughter:

> I have done nothing but in care of thee,
> Of thee, my dear one, thee my daughter, who
> Art ignorant of what thou art,
>
> (Act I, scene 2, 16-18)

This suggests selflessness as well as the unremitting concentration he has had to devote to bringing his enemies to the island. He has studied rigorously to obtain his magical powers, all the necessary branches of 'art', including the astronomy needed to recognise the "auspicious star" when it appears. (This may remind us of the New Testament magi who acted upon the appearance of a looked-for star. Some commentators honour Prospero with the title Magus). It is not study for study's sake but study in order to help make certain events come about. He has also followed the discipline (the island existence, of course, makes this a necessity – it also establishes the concept in our minds) of chastity, a prerequisite of those who would seek "the treasure of heavenly wisdom and knowledge". Moral purity, self-discipline as preparation for being given the gift and the opportunity to recognise and act at the crucial moment. And, of course, the proper accoutrements – the robe, the staff and the books themselves, which do not seem to be passive items but actively magical. There is no reference anywhere to where he obtained these. All of this would provide evidence enough for seeing Prospero as the good magician, a character thus sustained throughout the play. In contrast, Caliban is a demi-devil, whose (in the words of Anthony Harris, in *Night's Black Agents – Witchcraft and Magic in 17th Century English Drama*) "strand of humanity in his brutish form offers some hope for his redemption".

As for his enemies, it will lead Prospero to the judgement that:

> The rarer action is
> In virtue than in vengeance. They being penitent,
> The sole drift of my purpose doth extend
> Not a frown further.
>
> (Act V, scene 1, 27-30)

Having brought them into the circle of forgiveness, Prospero renounces magic and trades his robe and staff for a sword and hat, the symbols of temporal power. He promises from now on to spend two thirds of his thoughts on the government of Milan previously neglected and one third piously on his own mortality. We feel that he too has been forgiven, has served his span of time in Limbo. And in his *Epilogue* he acknowledges sin and error, using overtly religious language ... "prayer", "Mercy", "pardon'd", "indulgence" – this last being a deeply serious pun suggesting, in the definitions of *The Shorter Oxford English Dictionary*, "favouring forbearance or relaxation of restraint ... the action of indulging in some practice, luxury, etc. ... a remission of the punishment which is still due to sin after sacramental absolution, this remission being valid in the court of conscience and before God, and being made by an application of the treasure of the Church on the part of a lawful superior." It was, we may remember, the sale of indulgences that sparked off the Reformation.

All this is an acceptable way of considering the play. But does the text always support it?

One highly critical view of Prospero can be found in the Liverpool sailor-writer and political activist of the early decades of the 20th century, George Garrett. Muir mentions having read him. Garrett calls Prospero "a tyrant, a sorcerer, and cunning", citing for evidence the "viciousness of his first conversation with Ariel". This paragraph from his essay *That Four-Flusher Prospero* is worth quoting:

> 'There's no harm done,' Prospero has twice told Miranda. If the scaring of helpless people to such an extent that they believe hell is let loose is no harm, what is? A thunder and lightning storm at sea is a horrifying experience. Adding fire to it is an act of fiendishness. 'In every cabin I flamed amazement.' Everybody on the wrecked ship must suffer accordingly. They do, or why would they 'plunge in the foaming brine'? The rest of the fleet, believing the king's ship lost, are bound sadly home for Naples. What matter, so long as all this suits Prospero's purpose?

More pertinently, Anthony Harris' *Night's Black Agents* presents another view. He links Prospero to the Shakespearean theme of the ineffectual ruler, rightly accusing him of "culpable negligence", like the Duke in *Measure for Measure*, in the governance of his dukedom: "to my state grew stranger, being transported/And rapt in secret studies". (Doubtless this meant that he neglected his daughter too for the first three years of her life when she had waiting women to tend her). He over-trustingly gives up the running of the dukedom to his devious brother. He confesses all of this while at the same time excoriating his Machiavellian brother. Does he in fact share the hubris of Faustus by maintaining an intellectual arrogance, telling us that on the island he possesses "volumes that/I prize above my kingdom" … still using the present tense "prize"? The theme is not new; it is something Shakespeare had long been exploring: the tensions between public duty and private pursuits.

James I was fervent in his pursuit of those who performed with the aid of spirits, as Shakespeare knew when he wrote *Macbeth*. Is this why Prospero finally abjures his rough magic? Is Kermode right when he says in his footnote to "rough" that it means "Expressing itself in manipulation of material forces; unsubtle by comparison with the next degree of the mage's enlightenment"? Kermode calls the speech in which this occurs "a valedictory invocation" of spirits. As is well-known, Shakespeare is here echoing one of his favourite authors, Ovid (probably in Golding's translation of 1567). The lines are spoken by the witch, Medea, (niece of Homer's Circe, a sorceress who turned men into pigs). The associations in this speech are not wholesome ones: moonshine and the witching hour of midnight, poisonous toadstools and mushrooms, the bedimming of the sun at noon, setting the elements in a rage, the opening of graves and the raising of the dead. It sounds like a speech Sycorax might make. In Golding's translation we have the words "darken the lightsome Moone", a power Sycorax is said to have had.

This is not in any way to say that Prospero is evil, only that he is a tempted human being. There is clear enough evidence that he hates and reviles Sycorax's "earthy and abhorr'd commands", calling her "The foul witch … who with age and envy/Was grown into a hoop." It was she who imprisoned Ariel and he who rescued him. But the above associations are with *witchcraft*; the spirits are "night's black agents"; like Sycorax, Prospero sends for dew at the witching hour of midnight. Harris points out that like Faustus he possesses the art of invisibility and that his rituals are all – unlike the magic in *A Midsummer Night's Dream* – performed off-stage and all put into effect by Ariel. "We witness," he says, "the end results … of unseen practices". Ariel, for all his angelic-sounding name and his insistence to Prospero that he has "made no mistakings", doesn't mean he is necessarily an innocent sprite; there is the possibility of mischief. At one point he is addressed as "malignant thing". And we know he disobeyed Sycorax. There may be similarities between the magic of Sycorax and Prospero; what is stressed is not so much that they are diametrically opposite but that his is *superior*. She, having imprisoned Ariel, "could not again undo" her spell, something of which he is capable. Ariel, too delicate a spirit, refused to obey her "earthy and abhorr'd commands" but does obey (with some outbursts of impatience) Prospero (is it a matter of his *having* to?) Much of this requires our belief that what Prospero says is incontrovertibly true, not hyperbolic. For example, what credence do we give to his statement that Caliban was "got by the devil himself"? If we are to take this literally then Caliban is, strictly, a demi-devil, the acceptance of which fact must qualify whatever sympathies we may – and of course we do – feel for him. (He has, as Bloom puts it, "his legitimate pathos"). His mother, who worships a pagan god, may be associated with Arabian necromancy (she was banished from Algiers – though Kermode offers another suggestion, namely that there was "a town called Algher in Sardinia of which the ancient name was Corax"), and she has links with classical witches. Prospero, like her, threatens Ariel with imprisonment in a tree (in his case an oak, associated with sacred groves?); like her, he can make people mad, read their thoughts (Sebastian says of Prospero "the devil speaks in him"), can strike them motionless and assume invisibility. All of this makes Harris conclude:

> Prospero's magical practices, however elevated they might appear, are in the final analysis as damnable as the blackest witchcraft, and his only hope of salvation lies in their renunciation and a return to a life of prayer and faith in the forgiveness and mercy of God.

In other words, like Faustus, he has been 'ravished' by magic and the conjuring up of spirits:

> These necromantic books are heavenly,
> Lines, circles, scenes, letters and characters:
> Ay, these are those that Faustus most desires.
> Oh, what a world of profit and delight,
> Of power, of honour, of omnipotence,
> Is promised to the studious artisan!
> (Marlowe's *Dr Faustus* Act I, scene 1, 49-54)

The excitement we witness here was far from being an uncommon thing among European intellectuals of the Renaissance period. Part of this excitement lies in the finding of esoteric ways into gaining and being privy to secret (and possibly damnable) knowledge. This excitement animates *The Tempest* in that Prospero knows he is handling dangerous materials, that he is engaged in a balancing act. Those who see the play as a fable or fairy tale or a spectacle rather than a drama proper fail to register this tension. E.K. Chambers, for instance, maintains that Prospero's "practical omnipotence ... takes all vitality from the plots he unravels and from the conflict between hero and villain which they represent". Tension in the play comes from his knowledge that, having made all the necessary calculations, this particular day is make-or-break for him: he is to come face-to-face with his enemies, cement an alliance between Naples and Milan through the betrothal of his daughter to the Prince of Naples, release his faithful Ariel from further obligation, and regain his dukedom. All this depends upon his recognising an "auspicious star". As he tells Miranda:

> The hour's now come.
> The very minute bids thee ope thine ear.
> Obey, and be attentive.
>
> (Act I, scene 2, 36-8)

It also depends upon the magic working and on the effectiveness of Ariel in fulfilling his commands. It is a truism that if you would like to be lucky you have to put yourself in the way of it.

With this view of Prospero as human, as someone who acknowledges his own darkness, and not a Disney version of Merlin or a benevolent Father Christmas, we can see him more as an individual, like Faustus, tempted by esoteric knowledge, punished for it (12 years on an island), hoping to put what art he has acquired to the service of the good and in the end asking to be "reliev'd by prayer,/Which pierces so, that it assaults/Mercy itself, and frees all faults." With it also we can understand perhaps what Kott meant in calling the play "a drama of men of the Renaissance", with Prospero a representative of "man the measure of all things", at a time when new philosophies were calling all in doubt. "The great dreams of the humanists about a happy era," says Kott, "had not been fulfilled: they turned out to be just a dream."

5

A Prince Of Power

Do we accept Prospero then as a white (benevolent) magician –
engaged in what Kermode calls "the disciplined exercise of virtuous
knowledge" – or, see him, like Faustus, as a dabbler in the black
arts? Does the play give enough information for us to be certain
either way? His quest doesn't actually seem to be for "virtuous
knowledge", certainly not in Dr Dee's definition, of "God the treasure
of heavenly wisdom" by someone who has "fallen in love with truth
and virtue ... (and) will for the rest of their lives devote their entire
energy to the pursuit of philosophy, whilst others (ensnared by the
enticements of this world or burning with a desire for riches) cannot
but devote all their energies to a life of pleasure and profit." Faustus
found it difficult to make the distinction: he becomes quite giddy
with the idea of acquiring knowledge and (a quandary scientists too
often find themselves in) of thinking how to apply it. Dee's pejorative
"pleasure and profit" reminds us of Faustus' "world of profit and
delight" promised to the "studious artisan". Prospero's admission to
being "transported/And rapt in secret studies" reminds us of Faustus'
quasi-sexual excitement in his line "'Tis magic, magic that hath
ravished me" (my italics). Banquo uses the word "rapt" to describe
Macbeth's fascinated attention to the pronouncements of the three
witches. There are suggestions of something trance-like and of being
ensnared. There are clear indications that Prospero is in thrall to
something he does not or cannot reveal to us: his inability or
reluctance, in the space of 12 years, to fit Miranda into her history,
for example, shows that he is either under orders of some kind and/
or it is because his books and his own calculations tell him he must
wait for a sign, for the "auspicious star".

Perhaps the nature of Prospero's art will have to remain
unsatisfyingly mysterious: the promise to explain things he gives to

Alonso at the end never comes our way. It belongs outside the play as a series of questions the audience take home with them. We know he can make spirits appear and make them do his bidding; we know too that his daughter understands he possesses this power ("If by your Art, my dearest father ..."). Caliban understands it too: in the plot to kill Prospero, he insists that his books are seized first. What power Prospero has – and it is considerable – has come directly from "secret studies"; he has neglected and therefore, one may argue, forfeited his reputation for "dignity" and "the liberal arts", aspects of the temporal power he should have responsibly exercised as Duke of Milan. The result of this neglect is to allow the "evil nature" of his false brother to come into play, he who then abuses the trust placed in him and becomes "absolute Milan". In addition, this brother then engineered a humiliating submission to an enemy, Naples, on condition that Prospero is extirpated (literally rooted up, eradicated – he has already compared himself to a tree and his brother to a parasitical growth: "he was/The ivy which had hid my princely trunk/ And sucked my verdure out on't").

In simple terms, in the Renaissance there was a tendency to categorise men as either 'heroic' (men of action) or 'contemplative': the ideal being a combination of the two. In *The Tempest* the contemplative Prospero ("dedicated/To closeness and the bettering of my mind") requires spirits to enact what he wills. (Bloom asks what would Ariel have done if Prospero hadn't roused himself at the memory of Caliban's plot against him ... and its corollary, "was the danger of Caliban's plot more real than many critics concede?")

The outward symbols of Prospero's magic are his robe, his staff, the books which (he confesses he *still* values them above his dukedom) he keeps in his cell, and – to him and the audience but to no-one else – the appearance and activity of Ariel and his gang of spirits. The laying aside of robe and staff suggests that his magic can be, as it were, deactivated. But is this entirely the case? Finally determining to give Miranda her own narrative (after 12 years' mysterious hesitation – "You have often/Begun to tell me what I am, but stopp'd,/And left me to a bootless inquisition") and therefore, at a critical moment in her life, gifting her with an extension to her sense of self, he says:

> 'Tis time
> I should inform thee farther. Lend thy hand
> And pluck my magic garment from me. – So,
> Lie there, my art.
>
> (Act I, scene 2, 24-5)

Much now depends on how we interpret his "Now I arise" at line 169. Does it mean he resumes his robe in order to put his daughter to sleep or does it simply mean things are looking good for him, are on the up-and-up? If the latter, does he (though there's no stage direction) put his robe back on just before saying:

> Here cease more questions.
> Thou art inclined to sleep. 'Tis a good dullness,
> And give it way. I know thou canst not choose.
>
> (Act I, scene 2, 184-6)

(This final clause is problematic if we apply it to all of the actions of the play). If the former, has he learnt the art of hypnosis and is this independent of his magical studies?

The major outcome of Prospero's magic is of course the storm, in which no-one is hurt. Not even clothes are touched. Gonzalo remarks:

> … our garments, being, as they were,
> Drenched in the sea, hold, notwithstanding, their
> Freshness and glosses, being rather new-dyed than
> Stained with salt water.
>
> (Act II, scene 1, 64-7)

The storm is real enough for those who endure it, as it is for Miranda, who says:

> The sky it seems would pour down stinking pitch,
> But that the sea, mounting to th' welkin's cheek,
> Dashes the fire out.
>
> (Act I, scene 2, 3-5)

(Notice the two elements of fire and water, with which Ariel is consistently associated, and remember ordeal by either of them either destroys or purifies).

One way of looking at the storm is to see it, as does Coleridge, as "the bustle of a tempest, from which the real horrors are abstracted; – therefore it is poetical, though not in strictness natural ... and is purposefully restrained from concentering the interest on itself, but used merely as an indication or tuning for what is to follow." This is talking with hindsight: when the play opens we have no idea that it is a magically raised storm we are witnessing. It is seen by King Alonso as a test of manhood ("Play the men"); the fate of everyone depends on the "labour" of the sailors; the passengers are encumbrances ("you do assist the storm"); royal or courtly natures are not respected; we are in a balance between survival and disaster in which Master and Boatswain are more important, despite whatever signals mode of dress and speech may suggest, than any niceties of social position and breeding. Coleridge is right to the extent that certain ideas, which the play will develop, are here adumbrated. We notice Gonzalo as someone trying to maintain hope and Antonio and Sebastian as cursers and scorners (Antonio thinks the sailors are all drunk); we find ourselves subjected to frightful noises; and we end the scene with praying as a last resort. It is only in scene 2 that we discover that:

> The direful spectacle of the wrack, which touched
> The very virtue of compassion in thee,
> I have with such provision in mine art
> So safely ordered, that there is no soul –
> No, not so much perdition as an hair
> Betid to any creature in the vessel
> Which thou heard'st cry, which thou saw'st sink.
>
> (Act I, scene 2, 26-32)

... that is unless some director puts Prospero at the side of the stage and has him waving his staff about in the air while the storm is in progress.

In an on-line essay entitled, 'Shakespeare's – *The Tempest* – A Jungian Interpretation', Barry Beck claims that, as water symbolizes the spirit, so:

> the tempest is a disarrangement of that spirit. It is Prospero's wrath, his temper, anger. The island represents an enchanted locality where things do not work by the normal rules of time, space and physical action. It depicts the new unknown

'*undiscovered country*'; lands of Shakespeare's time. The rules
of the known world may or may not apply.

Well, yes maybe, that is if you are one of those seeking to interpret
the play in terms of symbols, as allegory of some kind. In other words
simplify it by translating it into something else. Working on our
'imaginary forces', it is a 'real' storm we witness: the shift to
something else, another level of consciousness, only comes once it
is over.

And while we are talking of way-out interpretations, those who
take the Freudian line say Prospero represents the Ego, Ariel the
Super-Ego and Caliban the Id. This opens up the notion, suggested
by such as Duffy, that, if Caliban is Prospero's Id, then the attempted
rape of Miranda represents his subconscious urge to incest. Even the
sensible John Wain, despite his statement that:

> It is not Shakespeare's way to give neatly defined answers
> that can be taken away and applied independently of the works
> in which they occur. He will teach general lessons, but he will
> not give blackboard answers to specific problems.

is tempted into the assertion that Caliban is "the Id, the unregenerate
lower nature, in the personality in which Ariel represents the
imagination and Prospero the driving intellect." He is sufficiently
circumspect to say, however, "I avoid using the formal classification
of Id, Ego and Super-Ego, which does not, I think, quite fit the picture
here."

To begin a play by representing a violent storm on stage is, first
and foremost, a coup de théâtre. Over in under five minutes, it takes
some staging. How it was done at Blackfriars or the Globe or at
court we will never know. As we have noted, *The Tempest* is unusually
detailed in its stage directions: our storm is "*a tempestuous noise of
thunder and lightning*" … which can, as we said earlier, create
problems. We also suggested at the beginning that Shakespeare
continually transgresses the line between what is real and what is
imagined. This storm is both real and one which, having heard
Prospero on the matter, we realise we have also imagined and
imagined as real. This ludic interplay between appearance and reality
runs right throughout the play: we are in an actual theatre which is

also a Theatrum Mundi. As Anne Righter in *Shakespeare and the Idea of the Play* puts it:

> The world becomes a shifting haze of illusions. Prospero is like a dramatist, contriving a play, but he himself is an actor in the drama as well, involved with illusion on its own level.

It is not difficult to imagine Shakespeare gently sending up, with a smile of amusement on his face, his own cleverness – into the bargain, taking a dig at the utopianism (and the myth of the 'Noble Savage') he found in Montaigne and, in the masque-scene, at rare Ben Jonson, while at the same time showing the classicists he can do a five-acter that obeys the unities of time, place and action.

6

Thou Must Now Know Further

A technical problem comes with obeying the unities, usually catered for by the deployment of a chorus (ironically in *The Winter's Tale* Shakespeare uses a chorus, not for the purposes of exposition but for the opposite reason of sliding over 16 years).

Scene 2 of Act I turns Prospero into a kind of chorus and there are those critics who find this clumsily done. How does one create dramatic tension in what is simply an expository or filling-in process? Is this Shakespeare showing his – by this time – very sophisticated audience and the world at large that he can do anything he likes in the theatre and that they and we are all participating in a splendid comic device? Or do we infer that Prospero is a garrulous old man, like Polonius? Shakespeare also uses this scene – in what one could argue is a fairly cavalier way – to put the audience's mind at rest over the matter of costume (Prospero and Miranda do not appear, like Crusoe, dressed in goatskins) as well as the matter of Prospero's supply of books. Good old Gonzalo, who has kindly furnished these things, even had the foresight to allow for 12 years of growing up on the part of Miranda.

Prospero is cued in by Miranda's horrified reactions to the storm – which she, like the audience, has been watching (is she too placed at the side of the stage while it is in progress?) – and what seem to be dire consequences for the people aboard the "brave vessel". We have dramatic interplay between her horror and his wish to allay it. It is at this point he takes off his mantle, as if signalling he is now acting the part of caring father rather than powerful magician, preparing to initiate her into the mysteries (another favourite interpretation of the play is to see it anthropologically as an initiation ceremony or fertility rite). So there is the tension arising out of the sensation that something momentous is happening ("the hour's now come;/The very minute bids thee ope thine ear") into which Miranda can now be admitted. Though we don't yet know it, it is the day of her betrothal to Ferdinand. Like a psychiatrist, he probes her mind for memories, so as to open up his narrative, while she breaks into it with questions and exclamations, with his interrupting it to accuse her of not listening. Either this is clumsy or a sign of his autocratic nature, or yet again, Shakespeare's gift to us of self-reflexive comic artistry.

Miranda's final question is of something we have perhaps been beguiled into forgetting: what was, after all, the purpose of the storm? We are now told enemies have landed on the island! (Those who consider the play merely a spectacle fail to register the anticipatory, sometimes nervy emotions Shakespeare has been creating). Prospero sends Miranda to sleep and begins the process all over again with Ariel and, after him, with Caliban.

Ariel reports on the effects of Prospero's "strong bidding" and extends our imaginative involvement in the storm, with his description of St Elmo's Fire. (We note the association of elements, fire and air, both of which significantly come from above ... to be set in contrast to Caliban's connections with earth and water). What animates the scene is Ariel's expectations of approval for performing Prospero's bidding "To the very article." This approval he duly receives ("Ariel, thy charge/Exactly is performed") but not without there being further tasks. Ariel extends his (I am using the masculine pronoun merely out of convenience, since Ariel, being spirit, is genderless and sexless) sense of anticipation to reminding his master of a promise ("Thou did promise/To bate me a full year"). He too is excited by prospects, thinking *his* hour's near when he will be granted his promised freedom, something he clearly feels he has earned:

> Remember I have done thee worthy service,
> Told thee no lies, made thee no mistakings, served
> Without or grudge or grumblings.
> (Act I, scene 2, 247-9)

The tension that both characters (if one can describe Ariel as a character) feel can be attributed to a clash of two very different but no less momentous sets of anticipations. Prospero's reactions to Ariel's requests are violent. His outburst, "Thou liest, malignant thing!" not only allows the history of Ariel to be told but should remind us of Sebastian's and Antonio's curses in scene 1, as well as being something to keep in mind when we hear Caliban's:

> You taught me language, and my profit on't
> Is, I know how to curse.
>
> (Act I, scene 2, 363-4)

And what – especially in view of the fact that some critics maintain Ariel is an angelic spirit – do we make of a magician calling his angelic 'familiar' a "malignant thing"? For both of them this is an important and possibly perilous day.

Caliban makes himself known to us first as a disembodied voice ("There's wood enough within" – with a possible pun on "wood" meaning "mad") responding to Prospero's insults ("Thou earth ... thou tortoise"). We are already programmed to expect something with evil associations from the account given of his mother, Sycorax, and Prospero's word "slave" and Miranda's "villain". In the strangely-named *Names of the Actors*, he is defined by the words "a savage and deformed slave" (for a full discussion of this see Kermode's *Introduction* to his Arden edition of the play). And here is one of those (politically incorrect) things to which we moderns have to make what adjustments we are capable of or are willing to. It is a sad fact that physical deformity was in Shakespeare's time equated with moral viciousness. We have only to remind ourselves of that arch-villain, Richard III, in whom deformity and evil are fatally conjoined:

> ... I, that am not shaped for sportive tricks
> Nor made to court an amorous looking glass;
> I, that am rudely stamped and want love's majesty
> To strut before a wanton ambling nymph;
> I, that am curtailed of this fair proportion,
> Cheated of feature by dissembling Nature,
> Deformed, unfinished, sent before my time
> Into this breathing world scarce half made up,
> And that so lamely and unfashionable
> That dogs bark at me as I halt by them.
>
> (Richard III, Act I, scene 1, 14-23)

Caliban comes in, ill-natured, cursing. His physical shapelessness (he is at one point described as a "whelp", something that needs to be licked into shape) reinforces the revulsion expected of us. He is immediately threatened with physical punishment ("that which we accompt as a punishment against evill is but a medicine against evill") as opposed to Ariel's "pains", which I take to mean 'hard tasks'. If language is power then Caliban's 'freedom of expression' amounts to little more than – in the present instance – curses. These provide him with the mere illusion of power: the rebel's spiteful but ineffectual answering-back. He has no alternative but to submit to a greater (some call it imperial arrogance) power:

> I must obey. His art is of such power,
> It would control my dam's god Setebos,
> And make a vassal of him.
>
> (Act I, scene 2, 372-4)

Prospero's magic has no control over Caliban's curses nor over Ariel's expressed desire for freedom. Both have, anthropomorphically, been endowed with human characteristics – frustration, impatience, the need for approval and for selfhood. Shakespeare has endowed them with consciousness and language. By the same token, Prospero is not an idealised being, whose studies have necessarily taught him self-discipline, but one with untidy emotions. Muir, describing Prospero as "an angry old man", considers the second scene of the play as exhibiting not "emotion recollected in tranquillity, but treachery recollected in anger". His nervousness about the coming events of the day is exacerbated by the 'moodiness' of Ariel and the surliness of Caliban.

It is after Ariel's compliant departure to become like "a nymph o' th' sea" that Prospero awakens Miranda. She is required to confront Caliban, the would-be violator of her honour. It makes for a contrast with Ariel's (with whom Miranda significantly has no encounters) musical ushering in of Prince Ferdinand and the exchange of eyes that seals her fate.

7

O You Wonder!

Critics may differ in their interpretations of Prospero, Ariel and – particularly – Caliban, but there is very little that is ambiguous about the rest of the characters.

Miranda we know is 15. Her name, as we have said, associates her with wonderment, admiration; it suggests innocent childlike vision. She is someone who not only admires but is the automatic subject of admiration. She is in some ways the princess of fairy story, whose hand in marriage can only be given to the suitor who passes the test set by her father, the king. Miranda's recent reconnecting with her own history suggests a rite of passage into womanhood and sexuality. Her memories of court life in Milan are so dim as to be of relatively little significance. There is no suggestion of worldly corruption. She has, perforce for 12 years, shared her father's life of chastity – or more accurately has been exposed to the model of chastity he embodies.

She has survived, with little or no memory of Milan, nor of the perilous sea journey undertaken at the age of three. Her father has educated her on the island and tells her perhaps a shade priggishly:

> and here
> Have I, thy schoolmaster, made thee more profit
> Than other princess can, that have more time
> For vainer hours, and tutors not so careful.
> (Act I, scene 2, 171-4)

To all intents and purposes, she might just as well have been born there. What her education has consisted in or for what purpose we have no way of knowing, unless it is a preparation for the union through marriage of Milan and Naples. It is certainly better than the average. She is, as Wain says, "the product of Nurture", someone of noble blood, whose education has clearly preserved her "pastoral innocence". And yet for her, as for everyone else, this is a crucial day of transformation. Into something rich and strange.

It would appear she knows nothing of Ariel but – and this is something she can only say after seeing Ferdinand – she does include Caliban as one of the only three *men* she has met, but not, ironically, before thinking Ferdinand is a spirit:

> I might call him
> A thing divine, for nothing natural
> I ever saw so noble.
>
> (Act I, scene 2, 418-20)

Here is the interplay of idealism and pragmatism. Modern cynicism is of no help, even when we sympathise with Prospero's:

> No, wench. It eats and sleeps and hath such senses
> As we have, such. This gallant which thou seest
> Was in the wrack; and, but he's something stained
> With grief, that's beauty's canker, thou mightst call him
> A goodly person. He hath lost his fellows,
> And strays about to find 'em.
>
> (Act I, scene 2, 413-18)

(Note the deflating word "wench" – though it is also possible to see this as a term of affection – and the introduction of grief as a "canker" that destroys beauty ... a line Blake surely knew and had in mind when he composed 'The Sick Rose'). Prospero is to repeat such sentiments later when Miranda describes the king and his retinue in terms of a 'brave new world', this time simply saying "'Tis new to thee." We nod the head wisely at these pronouncements while at the same time – unless cynicism poisons our attitude – honouring Miranda's innocent vision, one she has strangely maintained, despite the fact that Caliban has sought to violate her honour, an experience from which she emerges, like the people on board the tempest-tossed ship, with seemingly "no harm done". With a similar willing suspension of disbelief, we are required to believe in love at first sight – a condition with a magic of its own kind. It accords with Prospero's plans. In an aside he says:

It goes on, I see,
As my soul prompts it.

(Act I, scene 2, 420-1)

This looks problematic: has the exchanging of glances been the result of Prospero's spell or Cupid's dart? Some lines later Prospero is to say "The Duke of Milan/And his more braver daughter could control thee,/If now 'twere fit to do't" and again "They are both in either's pow'rs" suggesting a spontaneous event and something outside of his control. Coleridge sees it this way:

> In this scene, as it proceeds, is displayed the impression made by Ferdinand and Miranda on each other; it is love at first sight ... and it appears to me, that in all cases of real love, it is at one moment that it takes place. That moment may have been prepared for by previous esteem, admiration, or even affection, – yet love seems to require a momentary act of volition, by which a tacit bond of devotion is imposed, – a bond not to be hereafter broken without violating what should be sacred in our nature.

As Bloom tells us "*The Tempest* provokes speculation, partly because we expect esoteric wisdom from Prospero, though we never receive any." By the same token, it is difficult sometimes to distinguish what is happening as a result of magic and what is happening in actuality. But then, do we have time to play with such distinctions when we are sitting or standing in the theatre, absorbed into the collective consciousness of an audience?

8

So Noble

Ferdinand, like Olivia and her brother, Sebastian in *Twelfth Night,* is
the survivor of a storm at sea. He:

> With hair up-staring – then like reeds, not hair –
> Was the first man that leaped; cried, 'Hell is empty,
> And all the devils are here!'
>
> (Act I, scene 2, 213-15)

struggling with the elements and experiencing an infernal vision of
being snatched at by fiends. Was his leap into the sea an attempt to
save himself or a despairing act? The last we'd heard of the sailors
and their passengers was that they had nothing left but prayer.

Ariel's segregating him from his fellows allows him to imagine
himself the sole survivor and therefore filled with grief for the putative
deaths of his fellows, and in particular his father:

> The King's son have I landed by himself,
> Whom I left cooling of the air with sighs
> In an odd angle of the isle, and sitting,
> His arms in this sad knot.
>
> (Act I, scene 2, 221-3)

(A question the play poses but doesn't answer is – does Ariel
have freedom over the details of Prospero's behests? Is he really
only confirming events, spelling out the details so that his master
will be approving? Is it simply a means – like all the other moments
of exposition – to supply information to the audience? Prospero does
ask whether he has "Perform'd to the point the tempest I bade thee?"
to which Ariel replies, "To every article". A short while later Prospero
tells him "Ariel, thy charge/Exactly is performed" as if the plan and

all its details are Prospero's. But we cannot be sure. Is Ariel, like Puck, capable of error?)

There are, of course, two fathers in the play, both of them variations on the Shakespearean theme of the flawed ruler: Prospero who neglected the government of his dukedom to become "rapt in secret studies", and Alonso, his former enemy, who has made a mischievous pact with Antonio, Prospero's usurping Machiavellian brother. Both have virtuous children who will redeem them and dissolve enmity between them with marriage. Shakespeare, in his last plays, seems to inscribe hope for the world in the younger generation. A ritual belief in the power of virginity and chastity, as we shall see later, is a sine qua non.

The (princely) name Ferdinand, popular in both Italy and Spain, may or may not have had resonances for Shakespeare's audience. Naples, a possession of Spain with its own Spanish court, may have reminded them of the political and cultural connections between the two places. Alfonso was also a name of Kings of Naples. This connection would have also introduced into their minds the Mediterranean history of the Moors and the problems which that caused not only in terms of religion but also of trade. It was in an attempt to evade the Moors who blocked the way to the east where precious spices were found that mariners sought a western route and the New World momentously and incidentally was discovered. It was something from which Italy did not directly benefit, certainly nowhere as much as the countries, in particular Spain, to the west of them.

* * * *

Ariel, with the odd-sounding direction to "make thyself like a nymph of the sea" is told to "go hence/With diligence", presumably (does Ariel read Prospero's mind?) to lure Ferdinand by enchantments to his master's cell, a task he performs in the space of just over a hundred and twenty lines. Ferdinand is brought on stage by means of music, which as Congreve tells us "has charms to soothe the savage breast,/ To soften rocks, or bend a knotted oak." It is a strange music: Ariel's songs both carry a "burthen" (glossed by Kermode as "a continuous undersong") of menace: dogs barking, cocks crowing and death-bells ringing. Ferdinand's perception of this is different to that of the audience: he is mystified (cannot locate the source), thinks it part of a ritual ceremony to some pagan "god o' th' island", and yet talks about a "sweet air" with the power to calm the sea as well as soften the grief he experiences at the supposed death of his father. Here again is Shakespeare conflating real and unreal. To what degree is Ferdinand in a state of enchantment? Has he followed the music of his own volition or has it, as he says, "drawn me rather"? He is conscious of what is happening and can interpret it, as if in a state of semi-trance. Prospero tells Miranda to advance "the fringed curtains of thine eyes" so that she can now see properly. But what does she see? What she thinks is a spirit, a "thing divine". Ferdinand sees a "goddess". In the sophisticated world of courtly love these reactions, coming from Lysander, Demetrius, Hermia and Helena, would be part of a necessary word-game. Here, ironically, they are completely innocent. Straight-off, Ferdinand wants to marry her. The theme of how and by whom things are perceived (and their connection with poetry) is clearly a strong one in the play. As Coleridge says, "The power of poetry is, by a single word perhaps, to instil that energy into the mind which compels imagination to produce the picture."

In *A Midsummer Night's Dream* we are told that "Love can transpose to form and dignity"; it can also, as the comedies fully reveal, transpose to chaos and indignity before it finds "the concord of this discord." Love offered the possibility of an ennobling relationship yet, as the comedies show, too often first entering through the eye, creates a form of madness, the tangled web mortals weave, painfully emerging from which they are made to learn that "Love looks not with the eyes but with the mind." Love, at its best, is, as Shakespeare's sonnet 116 states, "a marriage of true minds".

Are we to believe that what occurs between Miranda and Ferdinand is love-at-first-sight, the instant here-and-now possession of an ideal? It is, of course, being made available to us through art, which teasingly requires us (testing our scepticisms) to wonder whether, (as we actually yearn for it to be so) it is possible in real life. It is Prospero's job to bring it into a reality (rather than, as in the comedies, through the lovers' progress through madness and error) where it can sustain the instant into and through the human conditions of everyday life ... and onward into eternity:

They are both in either's powers. But this swift
Business
I must uneasy make, lest too light winning
Make the prize light.

(Act I, scene 2, 451-4)

Like Blake, he knows that innocence has to make its way in the world of experience and, in order to do so, needs the aid of protectors. He is slowing things down and putting to the test … the test of his tetchiness and submission to his will, either by magic (as when Ferdinand raises his sword against him) or volitionally ("Might I through my prison once a day/Behold this maid: all corners else o' th' earth/Let liberty make use of; space enough/Have I in such a prison"). And so a Prince is gladly humbled into the fairy-tale task of carrying logs and is in the process ennobled. The contrast with the log-carrying of Caliban will be mentioned later. Maureen Duffy's Freudian view is that although Prospero knows that marriage "is the right course, emotionally he finds it almost intolerable and his treatment of the selected young man, Ferdinand, is a piece of humiliating sadism rationalised as testing him."

Miranda, of course, is also being tested in this new situation: her innocent credulity is jolted and, like Desdemona, she has to face the dilemma of a choice between a father to whom she owes obedience and the man who holds out the prospect of marriage. Though she may wonder, the audience knows that her father is ostensibly motivated by a purpose and proceeding out of love. They will remember:

I have done nothing but in care of thee,
Of thee, my dear one, thee my daughter

(Act I, scene 2, 16-17)

This "care" is to be put to the test and something that will bring a degree of parental pain.

The courtship scene, in Coleridge's view, is a masterpiece. We find Miranda, despite her father's orders, disobeying him. It is a necessary phase in her rite of passage into marriageable womanhood. Unlike Brabantio in *Othello*, Prospero, being a wiser parent, will hopefully master this. Ferdinand's proper insistence on her virginity, though perhaps odd to modern sceptics, declares his intentions to be honourable. Her role becomes progressively more pro-active. It is she who asks Ferdinand "Do you love me?" and actually the first to propose (though we know it is in his mind too):

> I am your wife, if you will marry me.
> If not, I'll die your maid.
>
> (Act III, scene 1, 83-4)

Given the sexual meaning of "die", the audience would certainly enjoy a joke here. And it is interesting that Prospero, overhearing their conversation, utters the remark, "Poor worm, thou art infected", reminding us of all those images of sickness associated in the comedies with the first throes of love. It is as if Miranda is now in thrall to a different infection-like magic which he has to watch over and control. Prospero, it seems to me, is in a perpetual state of what-if.

9

And Were The King On't, What Would I Do?

How many kings of or on the island are there?

Before we contemplate this, let's record that right at the beginning, in the opening scene, faith in the power of kings is undermined. Alonso and his courtiers are seen to be completely without influence in the storm; they simply get in the way of the mariners. (The Boatswain, even, seems to be more in charge than the Master. As with Alonso on the island, the Master is relatively taciturn, saying much less than his fellows). "What cares these roarers for the name of king? To cabin! Silence! Trouble us not", the Boatswain tells Gonzalo in response to his attempt to be helpful with advice. When all is up, those aboard are left with nothing but reconfirming allegiance ("Let's all sink wi' th' King") and prayers. The disordered elements have disrupted the hierarchical pattern. The Master and Boatswain only appear on the island at the very end of the play when order is completely restored.

Prospero rules the island with the aid of magic; Caliban lays claim to it thinking he should have inherited it after the death of his dam; Alonso is an actual king powerlessly cast up on it; Gonzalo cheerfully plays with the idea, in imagination, of being king of such an island; Ferdinand, thinking his father dead, assumes he is now a king but then, finding his father alive, becomes a king-in-waiting again; Stephano, with the promptings of Caliban, makes himself king; Sebastian, Alonso's brother, is involved in a failed plot to become king; Claribel is thought to live too far away as to have any claim on the throne of Naples. The themes of possession, usurpation, power politics and the use of force to gain and maintain power are clearly strong ones in the play.

Caliban, according to Kott, is "the rightful lord in the feudal sense", overthrown by Prospero, just as Prospero himself was by Antonio, his account of which is in Kott's view "a summary of Machiavelli's treatise, 'The Prince'." This leads him to the conclusion that "*The Tempest* is a great Renaissance tragedy of lost illusions." It also leads some commentators, as we have noted, to view Caliban as the native dispossessed by colonial adventurers, which others, like Bloom, see as wilful distortion of the play. Muir too is dismissive of this and other interpretations, stating that Caliban is not for instance a portrait of the groundlings of Shakespeare's audience ("Miranda being Shakespeare's poetry they sought to violate"), nor of the proletariat, "nor even a satirical comment on the rise of imperialism, the noble savage dispossessed by ignoble white men"; nor is he a Freudian "phallic demon … More plausibly Caliban can be taken to represent the animal nature of man, as the ordinary sensual man, as the mystery of antiquity, as Original Sin". We will consider more aspects of Caliban and the other kings – and would-be kings – later.

An irony – one that doesn't occur to Antonio and Sebastian when they plot to kill Alonso – is that Prospero's island doesn't make for much of a kingdom (on it Sebastian could only wear a hollow crown), any more than it could ever be a utopia anywhere else than in the mind of a sweet-tempered old courtier trying to maintain a desperate optimism. Ironically, it would be more suited to Caliban (that is if he had someone there with whom to mate) than to any of the other of the island's visitors.

At the theatrical level, we are watching actors jockeying for dramatic space.

10

An Airy Spirit

In 1588 Simon Forman wrote in his Diary "This yeare I began to practise necromancy, and to call aungells and spirits." Ariel is just such a conjured spirit – genderless, invisible to everyone except Prospero and the audience ... which means of course, if we consider the interplay of realities which activates this play, that other actors have to pretend not to see him. He is associated with the elements of air and fire, a jet-stream quickness of movement, and with music and strange noises. He suggests a kind of (illusory) freedom. The most active being in the play, he is free to range about. He has known confinement and therefore freedom is precious to him (can we say it is his natural condition?) He yearns for it and keeps reminding his master of the conditions of his service to him and therefore, by implication, the limits of his obligation. Is he an amoral being with a fundamental irresponsibility that needs disciplining? Given his freedom, would he be mischievous as Puck? (We know that at one point Prospero calls him "malignant thing" and threatens to imprison him again using the words "a torment/To lay upon the damn'd"). It is impossible to say. We only ever encounter him carrying out behests of Prospero and, outside of this, hear him voice his desire for liberty and witness the eventual granting of it. The question of what he does or would do with it is outside the range of the play.

(Caliban offers a contrast. For example it is possible to say that if Ariel is spirit, Caliban is animality, a being unable to rise very far above the sensual. Is Shakespeare asking us to contemplate how we, imperfect humans, reconcile the life of the spirit with the limitations of the physical? Is this reconciliation brought about in the marriage of Ferdinand and Miranda with its emphasis on chastity? There are, of course, bewildering numbers of interpretations made possible by this contrast – some of which have already been mentioned – such as: Ariel represents poetry and Caliban prose, etc. Jan Kott lists some of the many symbolic meanings critics have attached to Ariel – that he is soul, thought, intelligence, air, electricity "and even – in Catholic interpretations – Grace opposed to Nature". Each of these is obviously reductive).

We have already posed the question whether Ariel has freedom of choice within (general) parameters set by Prospero or no choice at all. In his reports back to his master he goes into considerable detail. Is this to tell Prospero what he, Ariel himself, has accomplished or is it simply the confirmation (the expectation of approval) of predetermined planning, the detail Prospero's, not his?

(The question of free-will in the play is problematic. Let's pose it with another question: are Prospero's enemies coerced by magical means towards repentance? We will raise this question again later).

Puck and Ariel are similar in several respects – in their invisibility, their ability to mimic voices, to lead characters to and fro. But the fact that Puck is capable of making mistakes, while Ariel answers to "every article", may suggest that Ariel is a spirit of a higher order, (some commentators suppose him to be an angel), one who, as we see at a crucial moment, like the Good Angel in a Morality Play, persuades Prospero into a forgiving mood. In this, his role is importantly pivotal. The obvious difference between Puck and Ariel is that the former thinks his mistakes are mischievous and amusing, while the latter is under obligation to get things right: his freedom depends on it and he has been threatened with re-imprisonment in an oak.

Harris, in his search for evidence to show Prospero's engagement with black rather than white magic, suggests that Shakespeare's audience might well have recognised Ariel as an "aerial demon", making the following observations: that Ferdinand declares, "Hell is empty/And all the demons here" (though this may simply be terror talking wildly), that, unlike Faustus (visited by Good and Bad Angels), there is no sign of Prospero having entered into any kind of pact with his 'demon' (unless, that is, we think there is something in his acknowledgment of Caliban as a "thing of darkness") and, whereas Mephistopheles tricks and deceives Faustus, it is Prospero who is in control – Ariel repaying him for releasing him from the cloven pine. Yet, as Harris admits, we never see Prospero performing any rites (beyond the laying aside and the putting on of his robe and the handling of his staff) or exercising magical powers (except for sending others to sleep and freezing their actions). We must assume these take place off-stage. What we do know is that Ariel, on his master's behalf, is responsible for the major events of the play. It may be said, of course, that Shakespeare is doing this so as to promote ambiguity. We have no way of knowing whether these rites are saintly or Satanic. It is part of the play's necessary dynamic that we do not know.

It is at the beginning of Act V that we see Ariel (and behind him "The good old lord, Gonzalo", whose subtle influence on the play cannot be underestimated) providing the play's dénouement:

> but chiefly,
> Him that you termed, sir, the good old lord, Gonzalo,
> His tears runs down his beard like winter's drops
> From eaves of reeds. Your charm so strongly works 'em
> That if you now beheld them your affections
> Would become tender
> *Pros.* Dost thou think so, spirit?
> *Ari.* Mine would, sir, were I human.
> *Pros.* And mine shall.
>
> (Act V, scene 1, 14-20)

I admit Prospero's "And mine shall" could possibly be taken to be a confirming of an already planned intention but the play becomes a more moving experience if we hear Ariel's sentiments (they seem to come right out of the mouth of *Star Trek's* Mr Data!) as turning Prospero away from vengeance towards compassion. This would certainly seem to be the case from the rest of his reply to Ariel:

> Hast thou, which art but air, a touch, a feeling
> Of their afflictions, and shall not myself,
> One of their kind, that relish all as sharply
> Passion as they, be kindlier moved than thou art?
> Though with their high wrongs I am struck to th' quick
> Yet with my nobler reason 'gainst my fury
> Do I take part. The rarer action is
> In virtue than in vengeance. They being penitent,
> The sole drift of my purpose doth extend
> Not a frown further.
>
> (Act V, scene 1, 21-30)

At the end of the play Prospero is delighted with Ariel. No longer is he a "malignant thing" but has become "My tricksy spirit". Ariel's final words are – like those of an actor wondering about the effectiveness of his performance – "Was't well done?" to which he receives the answer "Bravely, my diligence. Thou shalt be free." He is sent off to "Set Caliban and his companions free;/Untie the spell." Successfully returned, he is addressed, again affectionately, as "My Ariel, chick" and finally freed to the elements, his duties and obligations completed.

In the final analysis, as Kott reminds us, Ariel is just an actor on a stage and, deploring the way some directors project him as a capering Victorian fairy or a mincing dancer out of a bad performance of *Swan Lake*, suggests he "must not dance or run. He should move very slowly. He should stand still as often as possible. Only then can he become faster than thought."

11

Caliban My Slave

Most of the play's scenes are constructed using a character which has power and can wield it and another person or other people subject to it. A theme of the play then may be said to be the relationship between master and servant, especially when the relationship is strained. We have already noticed something of this in the storm scene where the Boatswain rages against the ineffectual noblemen aboard ship. Something of the relationship between Prospero and Ariel has already been discussed; that between Alonso and his courtiers and the Stephano/Trinculo/Caliban farrago will be discussed later. We should remind ourselves that, conventionally, the relationship between father and daughter is, at this time, based upon obedience, likewise between husband and wife; that younger brothers owe allegiance to their older brothers – remembering that, strictly, all of them are part of a highly organised hierarchy. This is not to ignore the fact that Shakespeare raises questions about such conventions, as for example with Desdemona or Ophelia with their respective fathers.

Despite the fact that he only speaks about 100 lines, the way we interpret Caliban will affect our view of the play as a whole. Put at its simplest, the choice is between seeing him as either a "thing most brutish" (a "born devil, on whose nature/Nurture can never stick") or as someone made that way by ill-treatment. ("For I am all the subjects that you have,/Which first was mine own king; and here you sty me/ In this hard rock, whiles you do keep from me/The rest o' th' island.") The second of these has been a fashion for some years. Jonathan Bate, we will remember, stated that the choice was between 'Prosperian' and a 'Calibanesque' reading.

If we accept Coleridge's view that "Shakespeare's characters are all … individualised", the question to be asked is what degree of individuality can we ascribe to Caliban. In Shakespeare's work there is nothing like him. He is, partly, fashioned out of seafarers' stories – in a word, a monster, invented to blur the distinction between man and beast. Trinculo tells us that in England people pay good money to behold such monsters: "There would this monster make a man. Any strange beast there makes a man. When they will not give a doit to relieve a lame beggar, they will lay out ten to see a dead Indian." In other words, Caliban to him is a commodity, a thing to be bought and sold, to be turned into a sideshow freak. An Elizabethan attitude to 'Red Indians' may be found in these words of Thomas Hariot (an associate of Sir Walter Raleigh and himself a noted magician, astronomer and explorer) quoted in *Elizabethan People – State and Society* ed. Joel Hurstfield and Alan G.R. Smith:

> In respect of us they are a people poor, and for want of skill and judgement in the knowledge and use of our things, do esteem our trifles before things of greater value: notwithstanding, in their proper manner, considering the want of such means as we have, they seem very ingenious; for although they have no tools, nor any such crafts, sciences and arts as we, yet in those things they do, they show excellency of wit. And by how much they upon due consideration shall find our manner of knowledges and crafts to exceed theirs in perfection, and speed for doing and execution, by so much more is it probable that they should desire our friendship and love, and have the greater respect for pleasing and obeying us. Whereby may be hoped, if means of good government be used, that they may in short time be brought to civility, and the embracing of the true religion.

Caliban has not much history to speak of and no real connections: his mother is dead; there is no tribe for him to belong to (unless it be the tribe of hell); his solitariness part of his uniqueness.

What history he can lay claim to we learn before we meet him on stage: it is mediated to us as part of Ariel's history – of which Prospero has to remind his spirit "Once in a month". He is "hagborn" from the coupling of a witch and the devil, a "freckled whelp" without human shape. Prospero and Miranda have attempted to educate and civilise him, only to be thanked by curses and the attempted rape of Miranda. Prospero has made him his slave and treats him to "cramps", "side-stitches", being pricked by hedgehogs and stung all over by bees. He is offered to us as unregenerate.

What are we to make of his complaints that the island belongs to him (this is true only in the sense that he was on it before Prospero); that Prospero and Miranda once treated him kindly, so that in return he showed them the good things of the island; that, in order to survive, ("I must eat my dinner") and because Prospero's art is so powerful, he must perforce obey – though doing it churlishly? His former benefactors' rage against him, at this juncture, is quite unforgiving: Caliban is a "lying slave", "filth", an "abhorred slave", "hag-seed", the personification of malice – one that expresses itself gleefully in:

> Oh ho, O ho! Would't had been done!
> Thou didst prevent me. I had peopled else
> This isle with Calibans.
>
> (Act I, scene 2, 349-51)

All that their kindness has done is to teach him to betray their trust and to curse. Whatever is (potentially) human in him, it may be argued, is expunged by his inhuman side. But isn't this often the case with humankind itself? It can be argued that, verbally, Prospero, in his rage, is an overbearing bully, more malicious than his churlish slave – that is unless we look upon Prospero as a (naturally) superior being and his rage as righteous indignation.

Later in the action, Caliban further degrades himself, with the help of Stephano's liquor (which he takes to be a god), into a drunken, servile brute and actually relinquishes his claim on the island to Stephano.

How do we square this with Coleridge's assertion that "Caliban is in some respects a noble being: the poet has raised him far above contempt"? The fact of the matter is that Shakespeare has teasingly given his monster some of the play's most memorable poetry. Coleridge says "he is a man in the sense of the imagination: all the images he uses are drawn from nature and are highly poetical; they fit in with the images of Ariel. Caliban gives us images from the earth, Ariel images from the air ... No mean figure is employed, no mean passion displayed, beyond animal passion and repugnance to command." Coleridge's "nature" is the nature of the Romantics, to whom it was teacher, nurse, inspirer, consoler. In this respect Caliban becomes a precursor of Mary Shelley's monster. But where Coleridge makes a pretty parallel between the imagery of Ariel and Caliban, Shakespeare understands contrast and opposition. This raises a problem. If Caliban speaks a poetry that appeals to the Romantic in us, whose poetry, we may ask, is it? The play's? The poet's? The character's? Ours?

These questions should put us on our guard when we perhaps too-readily bring sophisticated modern psychological interpretations to bear. Our Jungian critic tells us, "We all need an Ariel and Caliban in our Psyche ... (Caliban's) *Be not afeard* speech in Act III reveals him to be poetic, sensual, in tune with nature and naturally creative. He is also the physical strength of the island. We and Prospero need those creative, imaginative, brutish qualities as well as our intellectual, social, logical, conscious, ordered aspects ... Caliban is the *shadow* of the island and of Prospero's mind." Our critics of colonialism would say Caliban has the "pathos of exploited peoples". Bloom's verdict on this is: "Half a Wild Man, half a sea beast, Caliban has his legitimate pathos, but he cannot be interpreted as being somehow admirable." I am not, of course, denying the viability of such interpretations. The play has compass enough to sustain them. Indeed its emphases will always shift according to the spirit of the times.

An opposite view would be that of Kermode who confirms the attitudes that Shakespeare's audience almost certainly assumed – that Caliban is a repugnant character, depraved (his deformity being an outward show of moral ugliness), ignorant of gentleness and humanity, born to slavery not freedom, sprung from a "vile not a noble union", his parents signalling "evil magic" as opposed to Prospero's "benevolent Art" and the world of nurture, civility and "divine beauty." In a word, opposed to the Renaissance ideal of the pursuit of virtue and the belief that, in the words of Iago in *Othello*, "we have reason to cool our raging motions, our carnal stings, our unbitted lusts." The Attendant Spirit in Milton's *Comus* tells us:

> Mortals, that would follow me,
> Love Virtue, she alone is free.
> She can teach ye how to climb
> Higher than the sphery chime;

Or, if Virtue feeble were,
heaven itself would stoop to her.

And then, again, there is Kott's persuasion that Caliban – as the "greatest and most disturbing of Shakespeare's creations" – is a man not a monster. Doesn't Miranda include him in her statement "This/ Is the third man that e'er I saw"? And doesn't Shakespeare, more usually giving his low-life characters prose, honour him with poetry? Kott's conclusion is that he is "the most truly tragic" of the beings on the island, agreeing with Coleridge that he has "a full individuality". Caliban, he rightly states, "cannot be defined by one metaphor or contained in one allegory". In the final analysis, he is "just an actor wearing a costume"; he should be played as humanly as possible. Perhaps someone childlike, bewildered by the loss of his innocence, today's teenager?

And, of course, there is the interesting take on our "hag-seed" in Browning's exhilarating poem, *Caliban Upon Setebos,* as well as in Auden's *The Sea and The Mirror.* Auden once played the part of Caliban in a school production of *The Tempest*, a play whose conclusion he ended up judging, in the words of his biographer, Humphrey Carpenter, "inadequate for its themes". Carpenter quotes Auden as saying "Both the repentance of the guilty and the pardon of the injured seem more formal than real." *The Sea and the Mirror* reinterprets the play by presenting, in the words of another biographer, Richard Davenport Hines, "the Christian conception of art" and tracing "the kinship between perfect divine love and imperfect human love."

Note:

For a detailed account of the master/servant themes found in classical literature, to which Shakespeare was almost certainly indebted, consult Bernard Knox's essay 'The Tempest and the Ancient Comic Tradition in English Stage Comedy', English Institute Essays, ed. W.K. Wimsatt Jr., Columbia University Press, 1955.

12

Cold Porridge

Prospero is to exchange "fury" for "nobler reason".

The fury of the sea is allayed by music, as is Ferdinand's passion (his grief at the supposed loss of his father); and a motley crew is cast up on the island: the low-life comics, Stephano and Trinculo, who leaven the severity of the rest of the play with uproarious knock-about (at the same time, providing an ominous undersong that adds to the play's interplay of meanings); King Alonso and his courtiers, among whom are the perfidious brothers and the goodly Gonzalo – with Ferdinand cast up elsewhere in solitary wretchedness. They do not know it but they have been brought here, into a magic circle, for the purposes of (furious) revenge.

They are conscious of having survived the storm and are trying to come to terms with their new surroundings. Gonzalo is trying to make the best of a bad job but his attempts to cheer the King up fall on deaf ears and provide cues for the cynical Antonio and Sebastian to play spiteful word-games. In this, they are unwittingly enacting the role of court jesters (his majesty's corrupters of words), using the good old Gonzalo as their butt. "The immediate comedy," Bloom says, "is that Gonzalo and Adrian have the truer perspective, since the isle (though they cannot know this) is enchanted, while Antonio and Sebastian are savage reductionists who "mistake the truth". Compared to the slapstick Stephano and Trinculo, their species of comedy is slyly self-regarding, simply an activity (to take a phrase of Iago) to plume up the will. It is a form of indolence; it fills in the time: Sebastian admits as much when he tells Antonio in Act II, scene 1 that he is speaking a "sleepy language" and that "to ebb/Hereditary sloth instructs me." Life to such people is a game and idleness the spawning ground of opportunistic mischief. It is not long therefore before they are plotting murder and usurpation, repeating patterns of criminal behaviour with which the play is familiar, and they do so as if there is no tomorrow. But it is Shakespeare's purpose, in his last plays, to explore whether the good tomorrow is possible. Remember we found a hopeful projecting into the future in the *name* Prospero. It is not to be found in Gonzalo's utopianism, however attractive that dream may be, nor, as Prospero is to discover, in vengeance. It is certainly not to be encountered in the cynical world of Antonio and Sebastian nor in the drunken behaviour of Stephano and Trinculo, who are also murderous villains in the making. Prospero has let loose more than a storm on the island.

The early settlers of America fled a corrupt and sinful Old World in the hope of creating a new life in the New. They yearned to leave Original Sin behind them. This is the source of the American Dream that still activates much of American politics and culture – a belief that (to use the title of a Steinbeck novel) the pastures of heaven were theirs to inhabit. Of course, Original Sin, like the various diseases they carried, was imported with them and gave the American Dream its other face. This is what occurs on the island. Original Sin is introduced. What, we might vainly speculate, would have happened if a certain "rotten carcass of a butt" hadn't landed up there and, before that, Sycorax had not been marooned on its shores? Considering the first of these, would (though Ariel would still be pent up) Caliban have innocently ruled the island; with the second, would Ariel be free as the wind? Of course, these questions can only be asked. Sycorax (does she too count as a colonial – Moorish – imperialist?) did land there and did bear Caliban and did imprison Ariel in the cloven pine. The island on which Prospero and Miranda land is no Paradise: Original Sin is already active there.

*   *   *   *

One could argue that Gonzalo is the most important character in the play. Without him, there would have been no story. It is facile, as is too often the case with Polonius, to project him as a doddery and garrulous comic character and it is too easy to adopt – like Antonio and Sebastian – a cynical attitude to the goodness, cheeriness and patient restraint he offers the play. It is he who provides the positive undersong to the raging storm. His first words are "Nay, good, be patient". He is an optimist: "I have great comfort from this fellow.

Methinks he hath no drowning – mark upon him." And his optimism (and a faith in the "wills above") is, against seemingly impossible odds, repaid. He does live to "die a dry death".

When next we meet him – at the beginning of Act II – he is again typically trying to look on the bright side:

> Beseech you, sir, be merry. You have cause –
> So have we all – of joy; for our escape
> Is much beyond our loss. Our hint of woe
> Is common. Every day, some sailor's wife,
> The masters of some merchant, and the merchant,
> Have just our theme of woe. But for the miracle,
> I mean our preservation, few in millions
> Can speak like us. Then wisely, good sir, weigh
> Our sorrow with our comfort.
>
> (Act II, scene 1, 1-9)

This could be the voice of one of the earliest settlers setting foot on land after the long and perilous Atlantic voyage to the New World. Whether this optimism is something the play endorses is another question. Let's just say for the moment that, through him, we are aware of the presence of good on the island, which may reinforce – since Gonzalo is his friend and ally – our (uncertain) wish to think Prospero a good man placed there by "Providence divine." Prospero tells Miranda:

> Some food we had, and some fresh water, that
> A noble Neapolitan, Gonzalo,
> Out of his charity, who being then appointed
> Master of this design, did give us, with
> Rich garments, linens, stuffs, and necessaries
> Which since have steaded much. So, of his gentleness,
> Knowing I loved my books, he furnished me
> From mine own library with volumes that
> I prize above my dukedom.
>
> (Act I, scene 2, 160-8)

This can be viewed as clumsy plot mechanics (even to the point of supplying, as we've noted, costumes Miranda can grow into), the sketching in of necessary background information. It can also be seen as part of the creation of a narrative, a history ... in itself part of what seems to me a major theme of the play – progress to selfhood, the freedom to be. This is Ariel's great wish and Prospero's in the *Epilogue*. Remember that up until this important day Miranda has no history; this is the day she attains selfhood, gains her inheritance. This is the day, too, Alonso, Antonio and Sebastian will be offered freedom from guilt, the chance to create new selves; when Caliban and Ferdinand will be released from enforced slavery. It is the day creative unions and reunions are made possible.

Both Prospero and Sycorax were (before the play) meant to perish. Both however survive: she escapes execution because of her pregnancy, he (almost certainly, in the "rotten carcass of a butt" to which he was assigned, expected to be swallowed up by the sea) by virtue of the goodness of Gonzalo. Antonio/Alonso clearly didn't realise who they had entrusted with the job of being "Master of this design". Here we may note a degree of disobedience to authority, parallel to that of Ariel towards Sycorax and, again, to that of Miranda when talking to Ferdinand in Act III. Perhaps the play is saying that disobedience in the service of the good, the just and the true is a natural component of progress towards selfhood and freedom – to what has been designated the journey from soul to self, from the Medieval to the Renaissance. This transformation (*pace* the exhilaration it provides) is one involving loss and gain, angst and certainty, a shift from Blakean innocence to experience. This ambivalence, it seems to me, is at the heart of the play's concerns.

Though Shakespeare seems careful to avoid direct allusions to Christianity, the play is packed with indirect Judæo-Christian references. I have suggested previously that, among other things, the *Book of Isaiah* is part of its background. In Prospero's speech above, there is the word "charity"; faith is present in the trust in the "wills above" and in "Providence divine"; hope is present in Prospero's name. What happens in the play is acted out and judged in the eyes of the wills above, as well as those of the audience.

13

Gather To A Head

There are those who think *The Tempest* morally ambiguous or that what morality it has on offer comes from art and not justice. The artist/dramatist simply creates events such as the happy endings. Well – yes and no.

There is no doubting that good and evil are actively present on Prospero's island (evil arrived there before him) and that he stands (nervously) poised between them. He is not comfortable in his assumption of power over his enemies or his judgement of them. His motives are mixed. He is positioned at a fork in the road between the Old Testament eye-for-an-eye justice and New Testament forgiveness and turning-the-other-cheek. As Muir suggests, the play "belongs to the frontier between ethics and aesthetics, between the real world and the imagined world of art". Prospero acknowledges himself victim of grave injustice and wishes to set right the wrongs he has suffered. And yet he has largely brought his misfortunes down on his own head. His enemies, if they were so minded, could claim extenuating circumstances! But revenge, according to Bacon, is a kind of "wild justice"; not necessarily the same as divine justice. This is a subject explored in many plays of the period, most graphically perhaps in *Hamlet* and *King Lear.*

Prospero is furious with Antonio for his perfidy (it has been, we may assume, kept stoked-up during a 12 year confinement on the island) but seems to have no conscience about enslaving Caliban and Ariel. Is his sense of justice flawed? Are his actions simply self-serving? Providence and Fortune are, he claims, on his side and will work for him if he gets his calculations right on this day of the "auspicious star". A modern audience may think that this is little more than superstition at work in him. This is not the case: Prospero's diligence (a title he confers on Ariel) and his (sometimes stretched) self-discipline have made Providence and Fortune pro-active. But, being human and imperfect, he is, in this crucial instant, excited, nervous and therefore sometimes moody and cranky. His boat is coming home. Does it require us to believe in Providence, God's plan for the world? Is Shakespeare offering a meliorist view of human society? All's well that ends well?

But are the endings happy ones?

In Shakespeare's late plays people are offered second chances. If we take this simply as part of the convention of romance literature and of the (then fashionable) genre of tragic-comedy we are required to rejoice, to make our way home from the theatre in a glow of satisfaction that certain characters have been allowed to escape the comeuppance of poetic justice, taking with us the aesthetic pleasure of knowing everything has been beautifully rounded off. Whether our moral sense has been equally satisfied is another question. Much depends on whether we find the dominant pressure of the play is towards reconciliation, forgiveness. Our reading of *The Merchant of Venice* or *Measure for Measure* may be used to back this view, both being plays in which mercy and forgiveness are judged superior to the severities of the law and the "wild justice" of revenge. Duke Vincentio, for example, in the pardoning of others, achieves his own atonement. It also depends on our seeing Prospero as a judge representing human justice and reason and on our accepting the fairy-tale premise that they all lived happily ever after. For some audiences this will certainly be the case.

This is most obvious with the lovers. Ferdinand passes the test, is released from drudgery and Prospero, whilst insisting there is no pre-marital intercourse (a commonplace attitude in Shakespeare's time), happily arranges a celebration of the betrothal in the form of a masque, as a father's blessing. The burden of the masque he presents is one of fertility. This is the point in the play, noted by Frye, where we witness actors playing the part of spirits playing the part of the goddesses, Iris, Juno and Ceres who sing:

> *Honour, riches, marriage blessing,*
> *Long continuance, and increasing,*
> *Hourly joys be still upon you!*

(Act IV, scene 1, 106-8)

All very well. But if we follow Maureen Duffy's line we are obliged to see Prospero as "terrified that Ferdinand will seduce her (Miranda), although the rational father in him wishes them not only to fall in love but to love each other." She makes the point that he can always intervene magically if they try to get up to any hanky-panky. In any case, the masque is peremptorily interrupted when Prospero remembers "I had forgot that foul conspiracy/Of the beast Caliban and his confederates/Against my life." He has allowed his attention to lapse and his bad-temper (directed partly against himself) shocks Miranda: "Never till this day/Saw I him touched with anger, so distempered." It is at this point Prospero, a man knowing he is about to lose his daughter, delivers the play's most beautiful verse, which we will look at later. But let's note that an outcome of this speech is that Ferdinand and Miranda give him *their* blessing, saying together "We wish your peace". Are we to forget that Ferdinand had at one moment drawn his sword on Prospero?

In the final scene, Miranda and Ferdinand are 'discovered' playing at chess. Curtains are drawn to reveal an exhibition of a chaste occupation, an exercise in rationality. It is also to demonstrate to Alonso that he, as King, has been captured in a game of opposing forces, black and white. Alonso has been checkmated. But, in fact, he hasn't lost, rather gained the son he had thought drowned and now a daughter: "I am hers./But, O, how oddly will it sound that I/ Must ask my child forgiveness!" It must be said that, given the union of Milan and Naples signalled in the two young people playing chess, Alonso has no real alternative but to accept the situation, being unlikely to want to upset a dukedom to which his son becomes heir. But he seems to do so with a good grace. He too gives the couple his blessing: "Give me your hands./Let grief and sorrow still embrace his heart/That doth not wish you joy!"

But there is a problem. When the chess tableau is revealed we hear Miranda accusing Ferdinand of cheating: "Sweet lord, you play me false". What does this portend? Is this simply playful love-talk? Does it tell us that life ahead will contain – as it always does – disagreements and friction? Is this a relationship no different from others of its kind? Another point worth noticing is that the two of them do not immediately notice where they are or who is staring in amazement at them. Love is blind. A relationship built on hope that has yet to face reality. And yet it does feel as though Romeo and Juliet, as has been pointed out, have been allowed to live and marry.

But before all this, before we enter the magic circle of forgiveness, Prospero has told us that he is going to give up his "rough" magic. Does the word "rough" indicate a dissatisfaction that it is too concerned with violence or does it mean, as Kermode's footnote suggests, "unsubtle by comparison with the next degree of the mage's enlightenment"? In other words, that it has served its purpose? Or that the neophyte is giving up, faced with the next difficult stage on the road to knowledge? That he, Prospero, just doesn't have the strength and motivation to continue? Is the drawing in of his enemies a grand climacteric, a farewell performance? Is he saying goodbye to a former self, the one who once entertained the unsafe desire to isolate himself from the world?

Alonso enters the circle already chastened. From when he first appears in Act II we notice how little he says, how unresponsive he is to being cheered by Gonzalo's optimism or Sebastian's and Antonio's cynical drollery: he tells his courtiers:

> You cram these words into mine ears against
> The stomach of my sense.
>
> (Act II, scene 1, 108-9)

He already regrets marrying his daughter Claribel to the King of Tunis, blaming himself for the apparent consequences of this: that he has, in his own eyes, lost both a son and a daughter. Variations on the theme of banishment are played out in this scene.

The next time we meet him he has virtually given up hope ("I feel/The best is past.")

It is at this point (the disappearing banquet) that Ariel (not, significantly, Prospero) delivers sentence on him, Sebastian and Antonio as "three men of sin" (notice Gonzalo is excluded):

> You are three men of sin, whom destiny –
> That hath to instrument this lower world
> And what is in 't – the never-surfeited sea
> Hath caused to belch you up.
>
> (Act III, scene 3, 54-7)

The speech (is Ariel merely ventriloquising?) is harshly judge-mental. They have been made mad up to the point of potential suicide ("even with suchlike valour men hang and drown/Their proper selves.") and are roundly condemned. Ariel states that "the powers":

> do pronounce by me
> Lingering perdition – worse than any death
> Can be at once – shall step by step attend
> You and your ways; whose wraths to guard you from,
> Which here, in this most desolate isle, else falls
> Upon your heads, is nothing but heart's sorrow
> And a clear life ensuing.
>
> (Act III, scene 3, 77-83)

Their lives are to be purgatorial and their hope is to discover the possibility of living a blame-free ("clear") life from now on. Alonso's reaction to this is a despairing:

> (the thunder) did bass my trespass.
> Therefore my son i' th' ooze is bedded, and
> I'll seek him deeper than e'er plummet sounded,
> And with him there lie mudded.
>
> (Act III, scene 3, 101-4)

What is obvious in Alonso is the realisation, through loss, of love. At the end, in his joy at finding Ferdinand, he has the grace and humility to say he "Must ask my child forgiveness!"

It is interesting to note that the play mentions a son of Antonio's accompanying them aboard ship. Here we either have one of those anomalies where Shakespeare overlooks a detail or leaves it to us to assume the boy has been lost in the storm (though he'd be the only one who was!) and that Antonio's lack of thought for him, in contrast to Alonso's, merely underscores his callousness. If it is the former (something Shakespeare introduced but then forgot he had), then we simply see both Antonio and Sebastian enacting the roles of miscreant younger brothers, familiar to us from myth and fairy story. But *The Tempest* is not a fairy story any more than it is an allegory. Their what-ifs are malevolent (Traversi, in his essay in the Penguin Guide: *The Age of Shakespeare*, talks of their "ruthless egoism") and this leads Kott (speaking out of the ruins of post-war Europe) to the opinion that the play is "a drama of lost illusions, bitter wisdom, and of fragile – though stubborn – hope". It is significant, he states, that we find the word "despair" in Prospero's epilogue.

On the other hand, if these "degenerate representatives of the courtly sophisticated order" (Traversi) are offered entry "into a fuller life" we have no way of knowing that they accept this offer. Alonso tells Prospero:

> Thy dukedom I resign, and do entreat
> Thou pardon me my wrongs.
>
> (Act V, scene 1, 118-9)

Sebastian's reaction to Prospero is "The devil speaks in him." Antonio's response to:

> For you, most wicked sir, whom to call brother
> Would even infect my mouth, I do forgive
> Thy rankest fault – all of them; and require
> My dukedom of thee, which perforce, I know,
> Thou must restore.
>
> (Act V, scene 1, 130-134)

is total silence. This silence can be as sinister as Iago's at the end of *Othello*. Is it a refusal to enter into the circle of redemption? Only a director's decision can make this either way plain. He will either have Antonio shake his brother's hand or not. A production by Kott or one influenced by his writings would present us with a defiant Antonio. The emotional and aesthetic expectations aroused by Romance literature would require the former. But the play is not that simple. Bloom asks an interesting question: why "do Antonio and Sebastian, who express no repentance whatsoever, take no action against Prospero, if he no longer commands spirits?" Is it because "Prospero may yet attempt to abandon his art, but it is not at all clear that his supernatural authority will ever abandon him"?

Towards the play's final moments when Caliban is brought on stage, we hear Sebastian and Antonio in typically flippant vein. Their last utterances are to do with the possibility of making money out of exhibiting "this misshapen knave" as "a plain fish, and, no doubt marketable".

As for Caliban – he comes in hanging on to his mother's god, Setebos. His reaction to the assembled company echoes that of Miranda's earlier response: "these be brave spirits indeed", as if his master (Caliban notices that Prospero is dressed differently) has even more powerful spirits at his command. The sight of them and the fear of physical punishment cows him.

Prospero introduces him to the others as "this thing of darkness I/ Acknowledge mine". This is sometimes taken to be an acknowledgement of the dark element in Prospero's own make-up which he is now finally able to accept – his Freudian Id, his Jungian 'shadow'. It is something that deeply humanises him, makes him in Pope's phrase "darkly wise and rudely great". It is also sometimes understood to mean that he finally adopts Caliban, the failure to do so before this time helping to account for Caliban's churlishness. His master tells him:

> Go, sirrah, to my cell.
> Take with you your companions. As you look
> To have my pardon, trim it handsomely.
>> (Act V, scene 1, 292-4)

and receives the reply:

> Ay, that I will; and I'll be wise hereafter,
> And seek for grace. What a thrice double ass
> Was I to take this drunkard for a god,
>> (Act V, scene 1, 295-7)

If we compare this response to Alonso's and contrast it to Antonio's we cannot escape the conclusion that this is a kingly reaction. The 'better nature' of Caliban, which Prospero and Miranda had tried to cultivate, is uppermost and still viable; the Christian word 'grace' should not escape our attention. Wain records seeing a production of the play:

> in which Caliban, at the words "this thing of darkness I acknowledge mine", knelt to Prospero and received something like a blessing. Certainly the temptation, in this play, to conduct important business non-verbally is very strong for any director, whether in the theatre or the armchair.

It prompts the speculation: does Caliban go back to Milan with Prospero to continue his education and be "wise hereafter"? Bloom says "the thought of Caliban in Italy is well-nigh unthinkable". There is enough talk in the play of his being potentially exploited as a commodity (like a "dead Indian") on the mainland. And yet it doesn't feel satisfactory to leave him to his own solitary devices on the island, even if you are one of those who believe it his rightful property.

If we follow the notion that the play is about attaining selfhood or *amour-propre* – then Gonzalo's summing-up speech is important:

> Was Milan thrust from Milan that his issue
> Should become kings of Naples? O, rejoice
> Beyond a common joy, and set it down
> With gold on lasting pillars. In one voyage
> Did Claribel her husband find at Tunis,
> And Ferdinand her brother found a wife
> Where he himself was lost; Prospero his dukedom
> In a poor isle, and all of us ourselves
> When no man was his own.

(Act V, scene 1, 205-213)

Characters have volatile selves – moving in and out of illusion. Anne Righter is of the view that in *The Tempest* "The world becomes a shifting haze of illusions". And this prompts yet another difficult question hinted at earlier: to what degree does Prospero's magic affect the will? We know it affects *consciousness*, in that it can send people to sleep or freeze their actions; and Ariel tells the King and his courtiers that he has made them mad. We know for certain it can control their physical whereabouts. But we cannot know if the magic is coercive or what degree of freedom of will is available to anyone involved with it. The making Caliban churlish and Ariel impatient is, I suppose, part of any answer. But it is a fact that, as far as we can tell, Providence, Destiny, My Lady Fortune, the Powers Above and Shakespeare himself do, after all, construct the equation.

Perhaps only Ariel – like thought – is entirely free at the end.

14

Melted Into Air

Prospero's masque ("Some vanity of mine art") is a thing promised to Ferdinand and Miranda and expected by them. Ferdinand's response to it is that it is "a most majestic vision, and/Harmonious charmingly". It is a courtly entertainment, such as entertained James I, and some commentators think in it Shakespeare is parodying Ben Jonson, a prolific writer of these at the time, and some that it was incorporated at a later date for court performance. Be that as it may, the emphasis, as we have noted, is on fertility, an aspect of initiation into adulthood.

But, right in the middle of "a graceful dance", the dancers "to a strange, hollow, and confused noise ... heavily vanish". Order becomes disorder, as with the storm. It threatens Prospero's mind. He will need to take "a turn or two ... to still my beating mind".

He bursts into a rage that shocks the on-stage audience – as well as the real audience. Sensitive to this, he delivers one of the most beautiful and at the same time puzzling speeches of the play. Like Gonzalo with Alonso, he attempts to cheer his prospective son-in-law but, in doing so, almost dissolves the fabric of the whole play. It doesn't feel much like a cheering speech. Everything dissolves into insubstantiality. It leads Bloom to suggest that "what might vex the audience is that this powerful wizard is a nihilist, a kind of benign Iago ... whose project of necessity must end in despair". Anne Righter puts it this way: "The play and the reality it mirrors have become one, like the last paintings of Turner." (Kott thinks of the play in terms of "a system of mirrors ... both concave and convex, which reflect, magnify and parody the same situation.") It is what E.K. Chambers characterises as the "filmy texture of fantasy". Prospero's "cloud-capped towers" speech reads as if the mirrors have been washed clear of images. He is playing, he knows, a double role: that of leading character and that of dramatist of a play that has caught the conscience of a king. He is also, of course, an actor, a shadow, in a play in performance in a solid theatre in London on a particular 17th-century afternoon.

It is now time to draw it to its conclusion, to bring the curtain down. It is as though the speech is addressed more to himself than to Ferdinand. Is this what his studies have led to? The feeling that all, all is vanity, saith the preacher? "Some vanity of mine art". Is this a recognition of what the puritans keep maintaining, that fiction is a form of lying? That magic is sinful? Is this why the Epilogue asks for forgiveness? Is it the time for Art to hand itself over to Nature? For the audience to start thinking of going home?

This speech does not appear to be the thoughts of a happy man. It is not really the thoughts of a Christian either. "Our little life/Is rounded with a sleep" has no suggestion of resurrection behind it. It feels more like world-weary stoicism. And yet the play is about redemption ... but perhaps only in this life: "nothing but heart-sorrow/And a clear life ensuing". Prospero has promised to "drown his book" and, as we pointed out earlier, this singular "book" sounds odd when all previous mention of his studies has involved the plural "books". Bloom asks speculatively "which book will be drowned, out of the number in Prospero's library, or is this not his own manuscript? ... How can the magus, whatever his remaining powers may be, find his own in Milan?" (the phrase "his own" referring to the words of Gonzalo). Does Prospero cling on to others and take them back with him to Milan? Is the singular "book" no longer of use or is it too dangerous a commodity, evidence of sorcery?

Perhaps another way of looking at it is to imagine that, like the dying John of Gaunt, Prospero is in prophetic mode, opening up an apocalyptical vision of the coming of the end of the world. It is the job of the magician to tell futures. If we were superstitious we might remember the fire that destroyed the Globe Theatre two years later and, beyond that, the Great Fire of London.

Or yet again, if we accept the possibility of a Shakespeare in ludic mood, these lines could be played comically to tease the audience ... our little life being rounded with a sleep meaning that we are all going home and so to bed. The actors, revels over, are spirits (unreal) in the sense that they slip out of costume to become something else and also eventually go home and/or to the Mermaid Tavern.

Throughout his works Shakespeare plays theatre in-jokes and there are plenty enough of these in *The Tempest*. Many commentators stress the fact that, whether or not Prospero is a portrait of Shakespeare himself, he nonetheless acts like a dramatist, putting a play together, himself taking the leading part, just as (playfully) involved in the kaleidoscope of illusions as anyone else. It is in his Epilogue he seeks, like Ariel, his freedom.

15

Which Was To Please

It was a custom of the cast of Shakespeare's Company to end the day's performance with an on-stage jig or reel. It makes perfect sense. The dance acts as a safety-valve for all the emotions the play has aroused. The Greeks knew this too, ending the performance of sets of deeply affecting tragedies with a riotous, often bawdy satyr play. The actors, still in costume, are on stage as themselves – Burbage, Will Kemp, Robert Armin, Hemming, Condell, Shakespeare himself …

Before the dance, the audience is sometimes spoken or sung to directly: for example, Feste at the end of *Twelfth Night*, Puck at the end of *A Midsummer Night's Dream* and Prospero here in *The Tempest*, each of them sloughing off illusion, breaking the spell and soliciting applause.

We have noted the word 'shadow' as an epithet for actor. Puck begins his address to the audience with an in-joke "If we shadows have offended" and asks them to think they have been dreaming, and hoping they won't hiss ("If we have unearned luck/Now to scape the serpent's tongue") but rather applaud ("Give me your hands if we be friends" puns on shaking hands and using them to clap). Feste concludes his song with the lines "But that's all one, our play is done/And we'll strive to please you every day" – a bit of publicity for the company.

The play is over. Prospero has, so he avers, relinquished hold on magic (whether it lets go its hold on him is a matter of debate), perhaps realising in his phrase "rough magic" that life now requires another kind of knowledge. The Jungian view is that, having acknowledged his Caliban-shadow-unconscious, he "has taken a big step towards integrating his shadow within himself" and that in his willingness to abjure magic "is giving up his ideal utopia where he could define the rules and … will now rule others (and himself) as a mature human being." This is the process Jung called individuation. It is one (if we accept the importance of the theme of selfhood in the play) we may find ourselves having sympathy with. "Prospero has not only learned how to rule and forgive. He's learned to live with others and to know, recognise and accept himself. He's reconciled his two halves."

This, of course, is one interpretation among many. And as with any single interpretation tempts us with what may be partial and therefore limiting views. It is one that may require us to put a more idealistic value on political fairness, virginity, chastity, intellect and conformity than we are willing and thus undervalue pleasure, the imagination and creativity.

Wain puts it this way:

> this, as always, is Shakespeare's final word ... From 'art', even an art as great as his, we go back to the 'nature' of day-to-day living. The creative dream, the journey through the life-renewing region of the imagination, comes to an end, and we return, with new strength and new knowledge to the lives we live and the scenes we know.

Well, maybe.

Kott, on the other hand, wants us to see the play as being alive with the tension between "Renaissance idealism and scepticism, between a vision of order and one of chaos ... Prospero's staff cannot change history. When the morality is over, Prospero's magic power must also end. Only bitter wisdom remains."

*   *   *   *

The *Epilogue* is above all highly self-conscious theatre. The "bare island" reverts to being a stage surrounded by faces that need to emerge from the collective experience of being engrossed in a play and to have their individualities restored. They need to cooperate in the process of freeing themselves into this. Prospero (and the actor playing him) also requires permission to emerge from the dramatic spell with the help of favourable reception of the play ("gentle breath") and applause ("your good hands"). The purpose having been simply "to please" – which, in company with the aim of teaching, was the stated aim of art in the Renaissance. There is no doubting the fulfilling of the aim to please. What is less sure is what the play (implicitly) teaches.

I have admitted that, like many others, the romantic in me would like to believe Shakespeare is saying farewell to the theatre, to London and possibly to the court and perhaps to his old patron, the Earl of Southampton (Florio, the translator of Montaigne, being a friend of the Earl's and Southampton himself directly associated with the expeditions to Virginia with which Shakespeare is conversant). The main burden of the speech is that of being set free ("I must be here confined by you,/Or sent to Naples", "release me from my bands", "Let your indulgence set me free.") With these final words of Prospero we are left with (that is unless a flow of audience sympathy – unlikely to be denied – revitalises him) a frail old man, with no power other than what is left of his physical and mental resources to face the renewal of his responsibilities in Milan. Kott wants us to focus on the word "despair" but the word is qualified by "unless" ... "Unless I be relieved by prayer". The surface meaning of "prayer" is the plea to the audience he himself is making; it is also a request to be included in the audience's prayers. Prayer is another form of power: it "pierces so that it assaults/Mercy itself and frees all faults." Superficially, this is Prospero/Shakespeare asking for the faults of the play/performance to be forgiven; at a deeper level it is about the forgiveness of sins, the resurrection of the body and the life to come. Life after the theatre and life after death. It should remind us of Caliban's use of the word "grace". As a play is, in a sense, a bargain between dramatist/performers and audience, so too is prayer a two-way process:

As you from crimes would pardoned be,
Let your indulgence set me free.

16

Epilogue – Your Indulgence

Getting near the end of this book now, I'm beginning to feel like Prospero, wondering how best to emerge from its rough magic – to be free of it, drown it. Wondering too what life is going to be like the other side of it and whether good will come of it. Hoping – because I have offered a variety of interpretations – that I haven't created bewilderment or obfuscation. So many questions posed, so many of them unanswered. I did say at the beginning the play requires us to have open minds. In the theatre our attention is focused for us by the production, without, in Keats' famous words "any irritable reaching after fact and reason" on our part.

If I were to direct the play I would of necessity make directorial decisions on matters with which Shakespeare gives no help. I would be tempted in two ways: either to make a way-out production that took huge liberties or try to put on a sensible production that was as faithful to the text as possible and comprehended some of the things which I think might have been in it for its first audiences. The first of these would lead me into computers and virtual reality; the second, as you might be able to judge from whatever biases there are in this book, would show a Prospero dangerously dabbling in potentially damnable arts and concentrate on the playful way Shakespeare keeps reminding us that we are in a theatre. I would therefore want the Globe Theatre opened in 1996. I would be painfully aware that either of these would pin me down to *my* interpretation.

The aim would be, as it was Prospero's, to please. Or at least to find a way of balancing the play's tragic and comic elements. On the whole, I think I'd prefer my second choice, especially if I could work in the Globe, using (in the words of a good practical essay by David William, entitled '*The Tempest* on the Stage', found in *Jacobean Theatre: Stratford-upon-Avon Studies I*) the "inner stage for

Prospero's cell, the various galleries for Ariel as harpy, the appearance of Juno, the hell trap for the ship's cabins (and Caliban's rock?), and the platform for the main action."

People who attend performances at the modern Globe talk about being intimately involved in the play they are watching, about becoming part of the action. I would dress the actors in Elizabethan/Jacobean costumes in ways that indicated what William calls their "social identities". This also means that Prospero must have ready a costume that signals his resumption of his ducal responsibilities. Ariel must not be a Miss Tippy-toes; and Caliban must not be represented as a stinking fish. I prefer Kott's idea of Ariel as a young boy who doesn't delicately flicker and flutter about the stage but rather moves slowly; Caliban must be brutish but in a human way, not so grotesque that we disbelieve his "aspiration towards human nature". Like Jud Frye in the musical 'Oklahoma'.

My choice would be for a Prosperian reading. And he should be more man than Magus. I would have him eschew a big-voice delivery that would make him sound like a windbag. William commends the type of characterisation he witnessed in Gielgud in 1957: "Ascetic, wiry, and middle-aged in appearance, he admirably combined the three identities of father, duke, and magician." I confess I haven't seen Gielgud in the role but I doubt if I'd find myself as sympathetic: his delivery of Shakespeare's lines always seem rather plummy to me.

As for the seeming Puritanism of the play's insistence on chastity, William has a fine (relishable) pair of sentences. He says, "Nowadays, our attitude to the matter is supposedly more pragmatic. But in the 17th century glandular determinism did not enjoy the cultural ascendancy it does today."

If we determine that Caliban/Ariel are to be understood as "externalized aspects of Prospero" then we have to tread carefully so as not to give the impression we have imposed a formula on the play. William has this to say on the subject:

> It is, of course, very difficult, perhaps impossible, to suggest such ultimately abstract notions at all *specifically* on the stage. But one can suggest their *possibility*. That is to say, the appeal must be made to the imagination rather than the intellect. One cannot be too careful about introducing such notions into the

the overall concept of a production, but if such a triune relationship as I have indicated can be encompassed – and it can certainly be *assisted* by discreet costuming as well as casting – then I am sure it can only enhance the extraordinarily powerful impression which the supernatural element in the play is capable of making.

For me the play would be 'about' actively pursuing hope and grabbing hold of what goodness comes our way, however transient it may prove.

William's phrase "made to the imagination" is, I think, where we came in.

Bibliography

W.H. Auden, *Collected Poems* ed. Edward Mendelson (Faber, 1976), *The Enchafèd Flood,* (Faber, 1951)

Crystal Bartolovich's essay 'Baseless Fabric: London as a "World City"' appears in *The Tempest and Its Travels* ed. Peter Hulme & William H. Sherman (Reaktion Books, 2000)

Jonathan Bate, *The Genius of Shakespeare* (Picador, 1997)

Barry Beck, *Shakespeare's The Tempest: a Jungian Interpretation* http://www.wynja.com/personality/tempest.html

John Beer, *Blake's Humanism* (Manchester University Press, 1968)

William Blake, *Complete Poems,* ed. Alicia Ostriker (Penguin, 1979)

Harold Bloom, *Shakespeare and the Invention of the Human* (Fourth Estate, 1999)

Robert Browning, *Poetical Works 1833-1864* ed. Ian Jack (Oxford University Press, 1975)

Humphrey Carpenter, *W.H. Auden – a biography* (Unwin, 1981)

E.K. Chambers, *A Shakespearean Survey* (Penguin, 1964)

Samuel Coleridge, *Shakespearean Criticism* (Dent, 1961)

Maureen Duffy, *The Erotic World of Fairy* (Hodder & Stoughton, 1972)

Robert Foulke's essay 'The Literature of Voyaging' appears in *The Literature and Lore of the Sea* ed. Patricia Ann Carlson (Rodolfi, Amsterdam, 1986)

George Garrett, *The Collected George Garrett* ed. Michael Murphy (Trent Editions, 1999)

Richard Haklyut, *Voyages and Discoveries* ed. Jack Beeching (Penguin, 1972)

John Hale, *The Civilization of Europe in the Renaissance* (Harper Collins, 1993)

Anthony Harris, *Night's Black Agents – Witchcraft and Magic in Seventeenth Century English Drama* (Manchester University Press, 1980)

Richard Davenport Hines, *Auden* (Minerva, 1995)

Joel Hurstfield and Alan G.R. Smith (eds) *Elizabethan People – State and Society* (Edward Arnold, 1972)

John Keats, *Letters: a New Selection* ed. Robert Gittings (Oxford University Press, 1970)

Frank Kermode, Introduction to The Arden Shakespeare Paperbacks, *The Tempest* (Methuen, 1964)

Bernard Knox's essay '*The Tempest* and the Ancient Comic Tradition' appears in *English Stage Comedy* ed. W.K. Wimsatt Jr. (Columbia University Press, 1955)

Jan Kott, *Shakespeare Our Contemporary* (Methuen, 1964)

Christopher Marlowe, *Collected Plays* ed. J.B. Steane (Penguin, 1969)

John Milton, *Poetical Works* ed. Douglas Bush (Oxford University Press, 1966)

Michel Eyquem de Montaigne, *Essays* ed. J.M. Cohen (Penguin, 1958)

Sir Thomas More, *Utopia* ed. Paul Turner (Penguin, 1965)

Kenneth Muir, *Shakespeare's Comic Sequence* (Liverpool University Press, 1979)

Anne Righter, *Shakespeare and the Idea of the Play* (Penguin, 1967)

A.L. Rowse, *Simon Forman – Sex and Society in Shakespeare's Age* (Weidenfeld & Nicolson, 1974)

Sir Philip Sidney, *An Apology for Poetry* ed. R.W. Marsden (Manchester University Press, 2002); *Arcadia* ed. Maurice Evans (Penguin, 1977)

E.M.W. Tillyard, *Shakespeare's Last Plays* (Chatto & Windus, 1962)

D.A. Traversi's essay 'The Last Plays' appears in *The Age of Shakespeare: Volume 2 of a Guide to English Literature* ed. Boris Ford (Penguin, 1955)

John Wain, *The Living World of Shakespeare* (Penguin, 1964)

Marina Warner, *Signs and Wonders: Essays in Literature and Culture* (Chatto and Windus, 2003)

David William's essay '*The Tempest* on the Stage' appears in *Jacobean Theatre: Stratford-upon-Avon Studies I* ed. John Brown and Bernard Harris (Edward Arnold, 1960)

Benjamin Woolley, *The Queen's Conjuror – The Science and Magic of Dr Dee* (Harper Collins, 2001)

Frances Yates, *The Theatre of the World* (Routledge, 1969)

Editions used:

The *New Penguin Shakespeare* edition of *The Tempest* edited by Anne Barton. I have also had open on my desk the Signet edition, in which Bernard Knox's, Coleridge's essays and an extract from David William's are also to be found.

GREENWICH EXCHANGE BOOKS

LITERARY SERIES

The Greenwich Exchange Literary Series is a collection of critical essays of major or contemporary serious writers in English and selected European languages. The series is for the student, the teacher and 'common readers' and is an ideal resource for libraries. The *Times Educational Supplement* praised these books, saying, "The style of [this series] has a pressure of meaning behind it. Readers should learn from that ... If art is about selection, perception and taste, then this is it."

(ISBN prefix 1-871551- applies)
All books are paperbacks unless otherwise stated

The series includes:
W.H. Auden by Stephen Wade (36-6)
Honoré de Balzac by Wendy Mercer (48-X)
William Blake by Peter Davies (27-7)
The Brontës by Peter Davies (24-2)
Robert Browning by John Lucas (59-5)
Byron by Andrew Keanie (83-9)
Samuel Taylor Coleridge by Andrew Keanie (64-1)
Joseph Conrad by Martin Seymour-Smith (18-8)
William Cowper by Michael Thorn (25-0)
Charles Dickens by Robert Giddings (26-9)
Emily Dickinson by Marnie Pomeroy (68-4)
John Donne by Sean Haldane (23-4)
Ford Madox Ford by Anthony Fowles (63-3)
The Stagecraft of Brian Friel by David Grant (74-9)
Robert Frost by Warren Hope (70-6)
Thomas Hardy by Sean Haldane (33-1)
Seamus Heaney by Warren Hope (37-4)
Joseph Heller by Anthony Fowles (84-6)
Gerard Manley Hopkins by Sean Sheehan (77-3)
James Joyce by Michael Murphy (73-0)
Laughter in the Dark – The Plays of Joe Orton by Arthur Burke (56-0)
Philip Larkin by Warren Hope (35-8)
Poets of the First World War by John Greening (79-X)
Philip Roth by Paul McDonald (72-2)
Shakespeare's *Macbeth* by Matt Simpson (69-2)

Shakespeare's *Othello* by Matt Simpson (71-4)
Shakespeare's *The Tempest* by Matt Simpson (75-7)
Shakespeare's *Twelfth Night* by Matt Simpson (86-2)
Shakespeare's **Non-Dramatic Poetry** by Martin Seymour-Smith (22-6)
Shakespeare's **Sonnets** by Martin Seymour-Smith (38-2)
Shakespeare's *The Winter's Tale* by John Lucas (80-3)
Tobias Smollett by Robert Giddings (21-8)
Dylan Thomas by Peter Davies (78-1)
Alfred, Lord Tennyson by Michael Thorn (20-X)
William Wordsworth by Andrew Keanie (57-9)
W.B. Yeats by John Greening (34-X)

LITERATURE & BIOGRAPHY

Matthew Arnold and 'Thyrsis' *by Patrick Carill Connolly*
Matthew Arnold (1822-1888) was a leading poet, intellect and aesthete of
the Victorian epoch. He is now best known for his strictures as a literary
and cultural critic, and educationist. After a long period of neglect, his views
have come in for a re-evaluation. Arnold's poetry remains less well known,
yet his poems and his understanding of poetry, which defied the conventions
of his time, were central to his achievement.
The author traces Arnold's intellectual and poetic development, showing
how his poetry gathers its meanings from a lifetime's study of European
literature and philosophy. Connolly's unique exegesis of 'Thyrsis' draws
upon a wide-ranging analysis of the pastoral and its associated myths in
both classical and native cultures. This study shows lucidly and in detail
how Arnold encouraged the intense reflection of the mind on the subject
placed before it, believing in " … the all importance of the choice of the
subject, the necessity of accurate observation; and subordinate character of
expression."
Patrick Carill Connolly gained his English degree at Reading University
and taught English literature abroad for a number of years before returning
to Britain. He is now a civil servant living in London.
2004 • 180 pages • ISBN 1-871551-61-7

The Author, the Book and the Reader *by Robert Giddings*
This collection of essays analyses the effects of changing technology and
the attendant commercial pressures on literary styles and subject matter.
Authors covered include Charles Dickens, Tobias Smollett, Mark Twain,
Dr Johnson and John le Carré.
1991 • 220 pages • illustrated • ISBN 1-871551-01-3

Aleister Crowley and the Cult of Pan *by Paul Newman*
Few more nightmarish figures stalk English literature than Aleister Crowley (1875-1947), poet, magician, mountaineer and agent provocateur. In this groundbreaking study, Paul Newman dives into the occult mire of Crowley's works and fishes out gems and grotesqueries that are by turns ethereal, sublime, pornographic and horrifying. Like Oscar Wilde before him, Crowley stood in "symbolic relationship to his age" and to contemporaries like Rupert Brooke, G.K. Chesterton and the Portuguese modernist, Fernando Pessoa. An influential exponent of the cult of the Great God Pan, his essentially 'pagan' outlook was shared by major European writers as well as English novelists like E.M. Forster, D.H. Lawrence and Arthur Machen.
Paul Newman lives in Cornwall. Editor of the literary magazine *Abraxas*, he has written over ten books.
2004 • 222 pages • ISBN 1-871551-66-8

John Dryden *by Anthony Fowles*
Of all the poets of the Augustan age, John Dryden was the most worldly. Anthony Fowles traces Dryden's evolution from 'wordsmith' to major poet. This critical study shows a poet of vigour and technical panache whose art was forged in the heat and battle of a turbulent polemical and pamphleteering age. Although Dryden's status as a literary critic has long been established, Fowles draws attention to his neglected achievements as a translator of poetry. He deals also with the less well-known aspects of Dryden's work – his plays and occasional pieces.
Born in London and educated at the Universities of Oxford and Southern California, Anthony Fowles began his career in film-making before becoming an author of film and television scripts and more than twenty books. Readers will welcome the many contemporary references to novels and film with which Fowles illuminates the life and work of this decisively influential English poetic voice.
2003 • 292 pages • ISBN 1-871551-58-7

The Good That We Do *by John Lucas*
John Lucas' book blends fiction, biography and social history in order to tell the story of his grandfather, Horace Kelly. Headteacher of a succession of elementary schools in impoverished areas of London, 'Hod' Kelly was also a keen cricketer, a devotee of the music hall, and included among his friends the great trade union leader Ernest Bevin. In telling the story of his life, Lucas has provided a fascinating range of insights into the lives of ordinary Londoners from the First World War until the outbreak of the Second World War. Threaded throughout is an account of such people's

hunger for education, and of the different ways government, church and educational officialdom ministered to that hunger. *The Good That We Do* is both a study of one man and of a period when England changed, drastically and forever.

John Lucas is Professor Emeritus of the Universities of Loughborough and Nottingham Trent. He is the author of numerous works of a critical and scholarly nature and has published seven collections of poetry.

2001 • 214 pages • ISBN 1-871551-54-4

In Pursuit of Lewis Carroll *by Raphael Shaberman*

Sherlock Holmes and the author uncover new evidence in their investigations into the mysterious life and writing of Lewis Carroll. They examine published works by Carroll that have been overlooked by previous commentators. A newly-discovered poem, almost certainly by Carroll, is published here.

Amongst many aspects of Carroll's highly complex personality, this book explores his relationship with his parents, numerous child friends, and the formidable Mrs Liddell, mother of the immortal Alice. Raphael Shaberman was a founder member of the Lewis Carroll Society and a teacher of autistic children.

1994 • 118 pages • illustrated • ISBN 1-871551-13-7

Liar! Liar!: Jack Kerouac – Novelist *by R.J. Ellis*

The fullest study of Jack Kerouac's fiction to date. It is the first book to devote an individual chapter to every one of his novels. *On the Road*, *Visions of Cody* and *The Subterraneans* are reread in-depth, in a new and exciting way. *Visions of Gerard* and *Doctor Sax* are also strikingly reinterpreted, as are other daringly innovative writings, like 'The Railroad Earth' and his "try at a spontaneous *Finnegans Wake*" – *Old Angel Midnight*. Neglected writings, such as *Tristessa* and *Big Sur*, are also analysed, alongside better-known novels such as *Dharma Bums* and *Desolation Angels*.

R.J. Ellis is Senior Lecturer in English at Nottingham Trent University.

1999 • 294 pages • ISBN 1-871551-53-6

Musical Offering *by Yolanthe Leigh*

In a series of vivid sketches, anecdotes and reflections, Yolanthe Leigh tells the story of her growing up in the Poland of the 1930s and the Second World War. These are poignant episodes of a child's first encounters with both the enchantments and the cruelties of the world; and from a later time, stark memories of the brutality of the Nazi invasion, and the hardships of student life in Warsaw under the Occupation. But most of all this is a record of inward development; passages of remarkable intensity and simplicity describe the girl's response to religion, to music, and to her discovery of philosophy.

Yolanthe Leigh was formerly a Lecturer in Philosophy at Reading University.

2000 • 56 pages • ISBN: 1-871551-46-3

Norman Cameron *by Warren Hope*
Norman Cameron's poetry was admired by W.H. Auden, celebrated by Dylan Thomas and valued by Robert Graves. He was described by Martin Seymour-Smith as, "one of ... the most rewarding and pure poets of his generation ..." and is at last given a full-length biography. This eminently sociable man, who had periods of darkness and despair, wrote little poetry by comparison with others of his time, but it is always of a consistently high quality – imaginative and profound.

2000 • 220 pages • illustrated • ISBN 1-871551-05-6

POETRY

Adam's Thoughts in Winter *by Warren Hope*
Warren Hope's poems have appeared from time to time in a number of literary periodicals, pamphlets and anthologies on both sides of the Atlantic. They appeal to lovers of poetry everywhere. His poems are brief, clear, frequently lyrical, characterised by wit, but often distinguished by tenderness. The poems gathered in this first book-length collection counter the brutalising ethos of contemporary life, speaking of, and for, the virtues of modesty, honesty and gentleness in an individual, memorable way.

2000 • 46 pages • ISBN 1-871551-40-4

Baudelaire: Les Fleurs du Mal *Translated by F.W. Leakey*
Selected poems from *Les Fleurs du Mal* are translated with parallel French texts and are designed to be read with pleasure by readers who have no French as well as those who are practised in the French language.

F.W. Leakey was Professor of French in the University of London. As a scholar, critic and teacher he specialised in the work of Baudelaire for 50 years and published a number of books on the poet.

2001 • 152 pages • ISBN 1-871551-10-2

'The Last Blackbird' and other poems by Ralph Hodgson *edited and introduced by John Harding*
Ralph Hodgson (1871-1962) was a poet and illustrator whose most influential and enduring work appeared to great acclaim just prior to, and during, the First World War. His work is imbued with a spiritual passion for

the beauty of creation and the mystery of existence. This new selection brings together, for the first time in 40 years, some of the most beautiful and powerful 'hymns to life' in the English language.

John Harding lives in London. He is a freelance writer and teacher and is Ralph Hodgson's biographer.

2004 • 70 pages • ISBN 1-871551-81-1

Lines from the Stone Age *by Sean Haldane*

Reviewing Sean Haldane's 1992 volume *Desire in Belfast*, Robert Nye wrote in *The Times* that "Haldane can be sure of his place among the English poets." This place is not yet a conspicuous one, mainly because his early volumes appeared in Canada, and because he has earned his living by other means than literature. Despite this, his poems have always had their circle of readers. The 60 previously unpublished poems of *Lines from the Stone Age* – "lines of longing, terror, pride, lust and pain" – may widen this circle.

2000 • 52 pages • ISBN 1-871551-39-0

Shakespeare's Sonnets *by Martin Seymour-Smith*

Martin Seymour-Smith's outstanding achievement lies in the field of literary biography and criticism. In 1963 he produced his comprehensive edition, in the old spelling, of *Shakespeare's Sonnets* (here revised and corrected by himself and Peter Davies in 1998). With its landmark introduction and its brilliant critical commentary on each sonnet, it was praised by William Empson and John Dover Wilson. Stephen Spender said of him "I greatly admire Martin Seymour-Smith for the independence of his views and the great interest of his mind"; and both Robert Graves and Anthony Burgess described him as the leading critic of his time. His exegesis of the *Sonnets* remains unsurpassed.

2001 • 194 pages • ISBN 1-871551-38-2

The Rain and the Glass *by Robert Nye*

When Robert Nye's first poems were published, G.S. Fraser declared in the *Times Literary Supplement*: "Here is a proper poet, though it is hard to see how the larger literary public (greedy for flattery of their own concerns) could be brought to recognize that. But other proper poets – how many of them are left? – will recognize one of themselves."

Since then Nye has become known to a large public for his novels, especially *Falstaff* (1976), winner of the Hawthornden Prize and The Guardian Fiction Prize, and *The Late Mr Shakespeare* (1998). But his true vocation has always been poetry, and it is as a poet that he is best known to his fellow poets. "Nye is the inheritor of a poetic tradition that runs from Donne and Ralegh to Edward Thomas and Robert Graves," wrote James Aitchison in 1990, while the critic Gabriel Josipovici has described him as "one of the most interesting poets writing today, with a voice unlike that of any of his contemporaries".

This book contains all the poems Nye has written since his *Collected Poems* of 1995, together with his own selection from that volume. An introduction, telling the story of his poetic beginnings, affirms Nye's unfashionable belief in inspiration, as well as defining that quality of unforced truth which distinguishes the best of his work: "I have spent my life trying to write poems, but the poems gathered here came mostly when I was not."

2005 • 132 pages • ISBN 1-871551-41-2

Wilderness *by Martin Seymour-Smith*
This is Martin Seymour-Smith's first publication of his poetry for more than twenty years. This collection of 36 poems is a fearless account of an inner life of love, frustration, guilt, laughter and the celebration of others. He is best known to the general public as the author of the controversial and bestselling *Hardy* (1994).

1994 • 52 pages • ISBN 1-871551-08-0

BUSINESS

English Language Skills *by Vera Hughes*
If you want to be sure, (as a student, or in your business or personal life), that your written English is correct, this book is for you. Vera Hughes' aim is to help you to remember the basic rules of spelling, grammar and punctuation. 'Noun', 'verb', 'subject', 'object' and 'adjective' are the only technical terms used. The book teaches the clear, accurate English required by the business and office world. It coaches acceptable current usage and makes the rules easier to remember.

Vera Hughes was a civil servant and is a trainer and author of training manuals.

2002 • 142 pages • ISBN 1-871551-60-9